# The
# Christchurch and Bournemouth
# Union Workhouse

# The
# Christchurch and Bournemouth Union Workhouse

**Sue Newman**

Published by Sue Newman

© 2000 Sue Newman

**Second edition**

First published in 1994 by Sue Newman,
Fairhurst,
2 Magdalen Lane,
Christchurch,
Dorset
BH23 1PH

Tel. 01202 463373

*Winner of the David Thomas Self-Publishing Award (non-fiction) 1994*

This revised and extended edition published in 2000, as above.

ISBN 0 9524856 1 3

Second revised and enlarged edition.

(ISBN 0 9524856 0 5 first edition)

Printed, typeset and bound by
Chappell Gardener,
17 Haslemere Road,
Windsor, Berkshire, SL4 5ET

**Front cover:** *seal of the Christchurch Guardians, 1846 (although probably used from 1835): Public Record Office, ref. MH12/10711*

# Dedication

*Dedicated to the memory of The Christchurch Times journalists, without whose meticulous and faithful reporting this record of the affairs of the Christchurch Workhouse would be immensely the poorer.*

# *Acknowledgements for first edition*

I would like to thank the following for their contribution to this book, whether of information, photographs, advice or encouragement:

Mr Mike Allen, Mr Derek Beverley, Mr Gordon Bist, Miss Wendy Bowen, Miss Monica Brough-Slack, Miss Alison Carter, Miss Winifred Coffin, Mrs Grace Dargue, Mr Jack Dwyer, Mr Trevor Evans, Mrs Barbara Jones, Mr John Lewis, Mrs Charlotte Luckham, Mrs McGaw, Mrs Gladys Manton, Kathryn Morrison (Royal Commission on the Historical Monuments of England), Mrs Mabel Norman, Mr Joe Pilley, Mrs Violet Sawyer, Mr Ken Smith, Mr Ken Tullett and Mr H Weeks; also anyone else who I have inadvertently omitted from this list. One person to whom I am very grateful wished to remain anonymous.

I would also like to thank the following organisations which gave permission for material to be used in this book: *The Bournemouth Evening Echo*, the Royal Bournemouth and Christchurch NHS Trust, *The Financial Times*, the Dorset Record Office, the Ordnance Survey Office, and the Red House Museum (courtesy of the Hampshire County Council Museum Service).

## Additional acknowledgements for the second edition

The late Miss Ruth Abbott, the late Mr Richard and Mrs Diana Aldridge, Mr Nigel Brown, Mr Fred Blades, Mr C Cox, Mr and Mrs R Crockett, Ted Davey, Mr Tom Kelly, Ken Morgan, Elliot Newman, Mrs Christina Patrick, Terry Tuck, the Hampshire and Dorset Record Offices, the National Monuments Record Centre, the Public Record Office, the Red House Museum and Wiltshire County Council.

**Front cover design:** Elliot Newman

**Back cover:** Stained glass windows from the dining hall of Christchurch Hospital, recently reinstalled in the rebuilt entrance to the remaining buildings.

# Contents

**Abbreviations used in text or illustrations:**

DRO: Dorset Record Office
HRO: Hampshire Record Office
RHM: Red House Museum

# *Preface*

## 100 Years ago

### Sad Death of Little Girl
### Age 5$\frac{1}{2}$ years. Weight – 18lbs

On Tuesday morning an Inquest was held at the workhouse before Mr Bernard Hartfield, county coroner, touching the death of a little girl named Ethel Miller, aged 5 years, who died in that institution on Sunday last.

Mr A E Francis, solicitor, appeared to watch the proceedings on behalf of the local branch of the National Society for the Prevention of Cruelty to Children, and Police-Superintendant Haddon was also present. After the body had been viewed, the following evidence was adduced.

Inspector T Hunt of the Bournemouth branch of the NSPCC stated that in consequence of some information he had received, he visited a cottage in Pound Lane, Christchurch, on the 27th of March, accompanied by Police-Sargeant Hawkins. The mother of the deceased (Selina Miller) admitted him into the cottage, which was a four-roomed one. The deceased child was lying on a box, placed mouth upwards. There were nails driven into the sides and strings attached across from nail to nail. Over those was a small mattress, not quite the length of the box. On this the child was lying, covered up with a single sheet, one half of which was underneath the child's body. The mother said the father was upstairs, and he was called down. Witness asked the mother why she had allowed the child to be left in such a state, and she said, 'It's all right'. He (witness) said: 'Has any doctor seen it?' She said, 'Yes, Doctor Legate.' Asked when he first saw it, the mother said: 'The child was only taken ill seven weeks' ago, and at that time I sent for Dr Legate and he came once but did not come again for a month. At the end of the month I sent for him again.' Witness said: 'Why did you allow the child to remain here if you could not afford to keep it in a better condition, why did you not send it to the workhouse hospital?' She said: 'I don't want to do that.' Asked what she fed the child on, the mother replied: 'Doctor Legate is allowing me a pint of milk a day.'

---

The child appeared to be terribly emaciated and the surroundings as bad as it is possible to conceive. There was no fire in the place, no food that he could see, no furniture, the floor was damp and dirty, and the box in which the child was lying was placed immediately underneath the window. He (witness) questioned them as to their means, and the man said he could not earn very much. Witness's knowledge of his character was that it was not good; he could get drink very often. Witness told the parents that their want of means did not hinder them from placing the child where it would have comfort and attention. Witness asked whether there was no bed for the child to be upon and the woman said, 'Yes, but Doctor Legate says the child is not fit to be moved; it has to stay here day and night.' Witness went upstairs, but saw no bed at all. There was some cut straw upon the floor which had been used for sleeping on. The woman called his attention to some kind of tick that covered the straw, but she had taken it off to wash it. The man and wife admitted the child was theirs; they lived together but were not married. The child, though five years old, weighed only 19lbs. It ought to have weighed 40lbs at that age. Replying to the jurors, the inspector said the child did not speak to him. It lay quiet when he saw it, but when the mother moved it, it whined in a feeble manner. The body seemed a mere shell, and it lay crouched up with its knees almost close to its chin.

---

[Dr Legate testified that] in the interval before the 8th of March, the mother had again been confined. There was no one to attend to her except an old woman, and very probably the child had not had its medicine regularly. When he (witness) saw the child the second time it was lying upon some kind of covering on the floor. The room was very uncleanly and offensive. He advised the mother to get the place tidy and provide a bed for the child to lie on. The next day she had the child in a large perambulator.

---

About twelve months ago they had another child die in the lodging-house. They now had four children with them, including the baby. The child was very dirty when admitted to the workhouse.

*The Christchurch Times* 1894

The verdict was death caused by exhaustion following upon an abscess due to inflammation on the lungs. (The child, said Dr Legate, had had whooping cough followed by bronchial pneumonia.) There was a rider to the effect that the child's death was aggravated by the conditions of the surroundings.

This was Christchurch poverty in 1894.

It would probably have looked the same in 1794 or 1694.

*Chapter One*

# The beginnings

It has often been said that the poor are always with us. This was as true in times long ago as it is today; the attempts made by the authorities in Christchurch to alleviate the distress of poverty before the advent of the modern welfare state form the subject matter of this book.

It would have been the vagaries of the weather and the effect on the farming cycle that would have accounted for most of the cases of poverty in the town, depending as it did until the latter part of the last century on agriculture and fishing. Other sources of income would have been cottage-based. Predominant amongst these was the knitting of silk stockings, which was common in Christchurch. At the end of the 18th century, approximately 1,000 of the poorer women of the area were engaged in this occupation (according to *The Hampshire Repository*, which also records an early Aldridge by the name of John as one of the key employers). In addition to this there were other home-based industries – such as glove-making, spinning, and, of course, the well-known local occupations, the legitimate fusée chain-making and the illicit smuggling of contraband.

No specific national legislation existed until the 16th century, though the Priory Church certainly had a long and honourable record of assistance to the poor prior to the Dissolution, especially with gifts of food, and local charities were set up with the same aim of alleviating distress (e.g. White's Charity, Elliott's and, later, Coffin's charity).

Towards the end of the 16th century the parish, like all others in the country, was obliged by law to appoint Overseers of the Poor, whose task was to find work for those without and to construct a parish house for those unable to support themselves. These obligations were to be financed by the introduction of a Poor Rate levied on householders. Such persons that they were responsible for were only those from their own parishes; those from elsewhere were returned, using force if necessary, to what was known as their place of 'settlement'. This provision, further refined by the 1662 Act of Settlement, made lawyers rich in the ensuing centuries on the protracted squabbles between parishes anxious to avoid the expense of supporting a stranger, and was the cause of great social injustice; not the least of its effects being that those unable to find work in their home parish were unable to look elsewhere. Families could be split up, as legitimate children belonged to the parish of their birth, whilst illegitimate ones belonged to the parish of their mother's birth, not necessarily the same thing. Widows could also be returned to their place of birth. Beggars who arrived from elsewhere were liable to be literally whipped out of the parish: laws governing their control date back to 1744. All this would have made a person in dire need very wary of applying for parish relief. Although there did develop expedients by which a person could gain a settlement in another parish, such as obtaining employment for a year, it was never easy to attain, and in practice it was not uncommon for employers to sack the worker after 364 days in order not to create settlement rights for that person, which would have entitled them to parish relief.

*Notice of settlement examination, 1817*

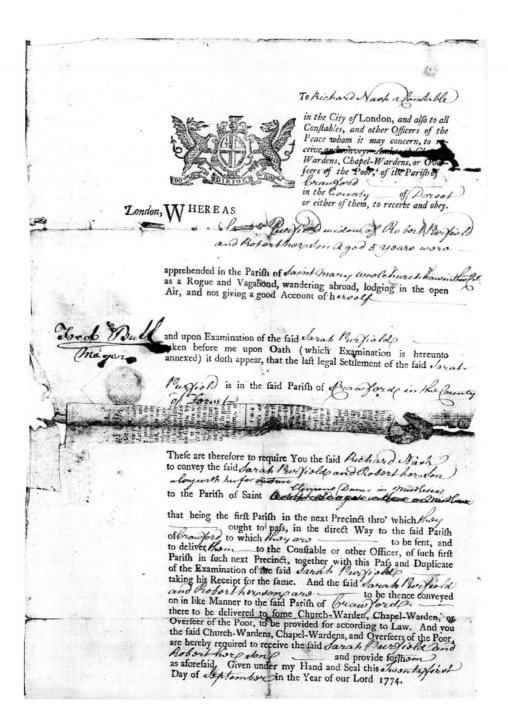

*To Richard Nash a Constable*

in the City of London, *and also to all Constables, and other Officers of the Peace whom it may concern, to receive and convey* ~~...~~ *Wardens, Chapel-Wardens, or Overseers of the Poor, of the Parish of* Crawford *in the County* of Dorset *or either of them, to receive and obey.*

*London,* WHEREAS Sarah Purfield widow of Robert Purfield and Robert her Son aged 5 years were

apprehended in the Parish of *Saint Mary Woolchurch hawin the City* as a Rogue and Vagabond, *wandering abroad, lodging in the open Air, and not giving a good Account of* herself

Fredk Bull Mayor

and upon Examination of the said Sarah Purfield taken before me upon Oath (which Examination is hereunto annexed) it doth appear, that the last legal Settlement of the said Sarah Purfield is in the said Parish of Crawford in the County of Dorset

These are therefore to require You the said *Richard Nash* to convey the said Sarah Purfield and Robert her Son along with her for nature to the Parish of Saint Clement Danes in Middlesex

that being the first Parish in the next Precinct thro' which they ought to pass, in the direct Way to the said Parish of Crawford to which they are to be sent, and to deliver them to the Constable or other Officer, of such first Parish in such next Precinct, together with this Pass and Duplicate of the Examination of the said Sarah Purfield taking his Receipt for the same. And the said Sarah Purfield and Robert her son are to be thence conveyed on in like Manner to the said Parish of Crawford there to be delivered to some Church-Warden, Chapel-Warden, or Overseer of the Poor, to be provided for according to Law. And you the said Church-Wardens, Chapel-Wardens, and Overseers of the Poor, are hereby required to receive the said Sarah Purfield and Robert her son and provide for them as aforesaid, Given under my Hand and Seal this twenty first Day of September in the Year of our Lord 1774.

*Removal Order against Sarah Purfield, 1774*

Illustrated on page 11 is an 1817 example of a disputed settlement case of a man with five children removed from Christchurch to Holdenhurst and notice given by the latter parish that he would be examined in front of the magistrates to determine to which of the two parishes he belonged. Also illustrated is part of an earlier (1774) document which somehow ended up in a private Christchurch collection, of one Sarah Purfield, detained in the parish of St Mary Woolchurch, London, as a 'Rogue and Vagabond', with her five-year-old son. To have been indicted as such she must have been in the class of vagrant who was a beggar who was cheating, 'a pedlar without a licence, or a Fencer, Common Player of Interludes, Minstrel, juggler, gypsy, fortune-teller' etc. Punishments could include a fine or a public whipping, but Sarah escaped these and was merely carted off to her presumed parish after an examination before the magistrates. As an example of the flimsy basis such decisions could be reached by, her enforced despatch to Tarrant Crawford was on the evidence that her father just might have been an apprentice there. As a widow, she had lost any place of settlement, obtained via her husband, although in this case he was Irish and never obtained one. Had she been classed as an 'Incorrigible Rogue', which charmless appellation was given to those whose offences included escaping from prison or refusing to answer questions from magistrates, she could have been transported. A lesser offence, merely unaggressive begging, or being workshy, was classed as 'Idle and Disorderly' – a bridewell punishment could be handed down. In earlier times, beggars could suffer even worse punishments – for instance, a hole made through the gristle of the ear, or for repeated offences, classed as a felon and hung!

Vagrants returning on their own accord to their own parish could be given passes by the magistrates: one relating to Christchurch for 1819 is illustrated. These allowed them to solicit alms lawfully.

It is against this general background that the building presently known as the Red House Museum came to be. The beginnings of this, the parish workhouse, have been documented in great detail by Herbert Druitt in the series of articles forming the *Christchurch Miscellany*, writing in 1924. He traces it back to a deed of 1745, when land in Comps Lane at the time, then occupied by a barn, skilling (shed or outhouse) and garden, was sold to the churchwardens and Overseers of the Poor of the parish. They had 'agreed to set up or open a Workhouse for the more comfortable support of their numerous Poor'.

It had seemed probable that this barn was sited at the corner of the present Quay Road and Church (Comps) Lane, on the site of the museum's art gallery,

*Vagrants' pass (HRO)*

13

but this suspicion was only confirmed by the recent discovery of the photograph reproduced on this page which is the only visual record of the barn to have come to light. It can be seen on the left of the picture, at the end of the brick-built parish workhouse which was later abutted onto it, and its original purpose has been confirmed by evidence in Public Record Office papers giving the dimensions of the rooms in use in the workhouse (in the mid-19th century) from which it is apparent that the rooms inside this part were 11' high. Plainly a barn, and presumably quite rudimentary – the deeds go back to 1711 – merely adapted for sheltering the poor and needy. The accounts for 1745-7 have not survived, but those of a few years' later have, and detail what appear to be extensive repairs of this 'Poor House', in 1759. Mention is made of all sorts of ironmongery and other items, such as 'rope yarn', 'tyle pins', a 'bushel of hair', 'spicke nails', 'oake timber, 'oake cantling', 'deal Baltic' and so on. Also, to 'trussing the ruff at the Poor House', implying a thatched building, as we would expect. A latch and bolt for a door, hooks and twists (to hang it) were also billed for. One overseer in his accounts for that year mysteriously itemises for 'Drawing a Plan of the Workhouse and attending to the Workmen on the repairs to give them directions according to my Plan and Estimate.'

Other accounts (1757) also refer to a payment to one Joseph Veal for 'watching two weeks at White Hall to prevent the smallpox, from spreading'. Another entry is for 'Charges on a Travelling woman called Jewel that was at Margaret Parsons with her Child the Small Pox being on the Child they were put to Whitehall November 19th 1757'. This suggests the existence of an earlier isolation building. Whitehall and Church Lane run into one another at the junction with Silver Street, and White Hall was certainly a building of some kind there, mentioned in a deed of 1814 as having by then been converted into three cottages. Its exact whereabouts is unknown.

Incidental information of a surprising nature is given in the accounts regarding the treatment of the smallpox, a very prevalent disease at the time. 'For Susanna Tucker and Jane Kendals charges in the smallpox, including butter, milk, cochineal, cinnamon, saffron, pomegranate, malt, sweet oil, treacle, wine, bread and apples, poppy-head, raisins, candles, one stick of liquorice and sugar candy. To the nurse attending on them one month, £1 10s.'

*The first workhouse: the converted barn of 1745, photographed 1870s (RHM)*

An entry in the overseers' accounts, dated 9 May 1763, next records the decision of the vestry to leave the 'whole management' of the conveyance of the new premises, as well as 'any controversy relating thereto', to a named group of local worthies. Dissension is thus hinted at, but about what is most unclear.

This reference in the overseers' accounts is to the construction of a workhouse: an entry in June 1763 announces that

> *the principal intention of the Parishioners in erecting a workhouse is to restrain and prevent Idleness and Vice, to encourage industry and good manners, and to lesson [sic] the heavy charges occasioned by the present defective method of providing for their Poor. Now to prevent any doubt hereinafter as to the nature and original design of this useful undertaking, it is … declared and Agreed that the said workhouse to be erected for the Habitation of the Poor, is with an intent that they may be more decently and comfortably relieved and maintained; that none able to do any work may any longer be maintained in Idleness; but that the Poor, who shall inhabit the said House may be properly and constantly employed therein, according to their respective strength and abilities.*

The previous month 40 guineas had been paid to John Willis for a tenement and garden 'in the road leading to the Abby … and which said tenement and garden with other houses and grounds adjoining … is hereby intended to be for the erecting a workhouse thereon for the use and better support of the poor inhabitants of this parish…' The fact that one Deborah Hawkins lived in the first property mentioned, and had to die before the sale could be completed, could possibly account for the rather curious appearance of the current museum building, which does seem to be in two parts, two similar but well-balanced sections, with a gap of continuous brickwork in the near centre. Architectural historians able to support or refute this speculation are invited to contact the author! Deborah Hawkins was still very much alive in 1764, since she was paid 'for her house room and for looking after Benjamin Bell when his arm was cut by an accident with a hatchett, 11s 3d.' So had her tenement already been pressed into service as part of the newly constructed workhouse, without waiting for her demise? At any rate, Benjamin seems to have received the best of attention, 'Sparkes bill for butcher's meat being supplied to him by order of the vestry at a cost of 11s 7d', and Dr Ayscough paid £1 4s for 'curing' his arm. Sparks was the name of a person who occupied timber shacks which once stood in front of the Constable's House.

Going back to the deeds before the workhouse was built, one dated 5 July 1763 describes the purchase of another 'messuage' and garden in the same street, by then known as 'Pitsdeep', in order to *erect* a workhouse. (A further confusing change of name is noted here: that in the latter part of the 19th century it was known as Mill Lane. Whitehall, its other road boundary, was known as Quomps Lane.) As soon as the purchase was completed, a committee was formed from the overseers and churchwardens, together with the 'Principal Inhabitants and Parishioners' (which august personages included well-known residents such as Charles Brander, Thomas Mews, Henry Mooring and Abraham Daw) to 'supervise the Purchasing building fiting up compleating furnishing Victualing and Governing' of the workhouse. This deed also records that 'the Poor of the said Parish were very numerous daily increasing and their maintenance very burthensome'.

To return to the post-1745 workhouse, it can be said with confidence that its life commenced 25 March 1764, for which date a Master was advertised for in *The Salisbury Journal*:

> *A Person fitly qualified to be Master of a parish Workhouse for the relief and employment of the poor, from Lady-Day next. It is expected that he be well recommended, and particularly for his Honesty, Sobriety, Diligence, and Temper.*

The pay was to be £30p.a. A Mr Bacon came forward, and the overseers made inquiries as to his character, but the *Journal* leaves us unenlightened as to his success.

A reference is then made in the accounts to a payment of 5s to Mr John Pardy for carrying turf to the workhouse (as fuel) 'to air it before the people went in'. Other items procured in the first few months were a motley assortment: brooms and earthen pans; a cap for a crippled boy sent to the workhouse; to an [illegible] man who took a lame boy out of the workhouse – 1s, and to the same person a pair of shoes when he left the

*The 1764 workhouse (RHM)*

parish, 6d; bushels of malt and hops, proving they made their own beer in the House (water in those days was wisely avoided if possible); 'for keeping Frances Rogers' children after she left them till they were put in the workhouse, 2s' (what a story that suggests) – later, her daughters were bought shoes and shifts; straw for bedding; filling five beds with hulls; wheelbarrows, sugar, soap, candles, rice; salt, starch and indigo (some sort of dyeing operation?); a 'lock for Mary Scott chained in lunacy'; sheets, 'blanketting', horn, buttons, canvas, shrouds, pairs of stays, pattens, leather breeches, sprig canvas, 36 ropes of onions, and so on. One endless fascinating stream of clues about the first occupants.

In the December of 1763, presumably whilst building of the new workhouse was underway, the harassed overseers were having to take legal advice on problems they were experiencing in collecting the Poor Rates:

> *There having been great remissness for several years in Collecting the Poors Rates for the Parish of C. so that the burthen of a numerous Poor lay much the heavier on such Parishioners as duly paid their Rates, a Resolution was lately taken to Compel the Payment of the arrears.*

The overseers went on to describe how magistrates' distress warrants had solved the problem, except in one case, that of 'a gentleman who having for Nine Years Evaded or refused Payment from time to time, under various pretences [and who] now threatens to Replevy [recover] the Distress if taken upon his Estate for the Arrears due from it, or to bring an action against the Officer who shall execute the Justices' Warrant.' Coyly identifying the culprit only by his initials, so afraid these officials must have been of reprisals (although it is apparent now that 'J. P.' was James Perkins of Winkton House, the rates due being for Winkton Farm), and frankly admitting that 'this Gentleman being of a very litigious turn', the overseers were advised they had very little redress against a landlord.

Reference to a Pest House appears in 1769 when two payments are made – one for smallpox at the Pest House, the other for *building* the Pest House, for which George Ward and James Letty were paid £69 15s. George Ward is recorded elsewhere as a carpenter; James 'Latty' as an ironmonger with premises near the

Market House (top of Castle Street). A pair of bellows were bought for it, 'necessaries' to do with smallpox treatment there, wood and turf supplies, bread, flour and 50 gallons of beer – all in the first year. In 1770 John Collins was paid £1 11s 6d for carrying someone to 'the hospital' by order of the vestry – a tidy sum. Many other payments involving the Pest House are made in these years: 1771 – Dr Henry Gibbs was paid a year's salary as surgeon and apothecary for the poor (£20) and a further £4 3s 3d for 'attending the people in the smallpox, at the pest house...'; 1778: 500 bundles of thatch sent to the Pest House, £6 5s; 1790: still more payments made for carrying people to the Pest House, plus, a 'gratuity paid to the Master and Mistress for their care and trouble attending the Small Pox people for the whole year' (three guineas).

Further research in the Public Record Office ledgers etc for the Union seem to solve the mystery, in that in 1843 the Guardians decided to sell parish property on St Catherine's Hill, comprising 'Garden Ground of half an acre with the bricks and building materials ... now untenanted, but late in the occupation of... two paupers, rent-free.' Their possessory title was said to go back 30 years, i.e. to about 1813. In all the resulting correspondence about the matter, especially concerning who owned the land it was on, as it seemed to have been built on the manorial waste, just once it is referred to as 'the Pest House'. Clearly, the Pest House was deliberately sited well away from the town in an attempt to prevent contagion, succeeding the mysterious White Hall.

Accounts may be thought to provide little potential interest, but those of the early workhouse years are a mine of fascinating insights into contemporary problems in everyday lives, the trouble the parish was put to in solving them, and the expenses incurred. Here are a few examples for the period 1774 to 1820:

1774: 'Paid expenses going to Southampton and taking up John Hogarth for deserting his family, and bringing him home, 5s 11d';
'Expenses in relieving and bringing home Elizabeth Gutheridge, a certificate person, £5 7s 7d';
1787: Penalty for not taking a parish apprentice, £10. Payment for taking one: £2;

*The Pest House*

1788: 'Paid expenses of eating and drinking, when apprehended Thomas Norris, who had deserted his family – 3s';

1789: 'Paid Francis Shearing to carry his child to the Infirmary, 7s';

1790: 'Paid expenses keeping in custody and conveying to the Bridewell at Winchester Peter Crabb for deserting his family, £3 12s 2½d';

'Paid Edward Tizard for carrying Flower Ford to London to an Hospital there, £7 17s 6d';

1791: 'Paid expenses for carrying three vagrants before Mr Willis at Sopley and afterwards passing them to Islington, 17s';

1791: 'Paid expenses at the Isle of Wight Hoy [in present Highcliffe] for a travelling woman taken ill there, 9s 6d';

1791: 'Paid H Humby for information and summons, being summoned before Mr Willis for refusing to relieve Ann Troke, 2s' [an interesting example of a relief applicant exercising the right of appeal to a magistrate on being refused parish aid];

1820: various interesting payments were made, e.g. to two sailors, a sailor and wife ill, a disabled sailor without shoes, a shoemaker ill going to Andover, a sailmaker, wife and child with one leg, three men seeking work, a sailor with a lame leg, a blind woman and man, a foreigner and wife …

Vestry accounts of 1792 refer also to the purchase of a cottage ' in the gravel pits … for the reception of such poor people of the … parish as shall not be thought proper to be received into the workhouse of the said parish'. Unfortunately, the records do not elaborate on the exact nature of the undesirable qualities of such people – whether they were vagrants, lunatics, or unmarried mothers we can only speculate. It is also possible that such people may have been infectious, a situation addressed in 1806 by the conversion of a room 'at the north end of the Poor House into a hospital for the reception of such poor people within the Workhouse who may labour under diseases of a contagious or infecting nature … It is agreed and resolved that the same shall be forthwith done in the least expensive way that can be.' (Vestry records.) This infectious ward was therefore in the old barn. It may be at this time that the Pest House was abandoned. Note the interchangeability of the term 'poorhouse' and 'workhouse' at this time. It was about the middle of the 19th century before the latter term took precedence nationally; poorhouses were more or less shelters for those unable to care for themselves, whereas workhouses were specifically intended to ensure that the inmates contributed to their maintenance through employment.

The plan opposite shows the ground floor layout of the workhouse – in Union times, it must be noted. It dates from 1870 (the 'Engine House' was a store for the parish fire engine), and it depicts the workhouse over a century after its construction, and may bear little relationship to the original layout and use. Nevertheless, it sheds some light on the interior arrangements. At the time of writing, more than a century further on than this plan, an entrance door to the museum comes into the men's wards, though now blocked; the hospital (barn) is now the site of the art gallery; the costume gallery occupies the schoolroom extension; and the women's wards, kitchen and stores have disappeared. The yards for men and boys are now a herb garden, the dividing wall having been removed, and the girls' yard and drying green are laid out with lawns and borders. A brick wall runs round the perimeter, very high on the Church Lane boundary, and a typical feature of workhouses everywhere. Such walls did not always prevent inmates from escaping over them: the most famous example is the great explorer, Sir Henry Stanley. Christchurch Workhouse had its fair share of dissatisfied inmates who 'ran off or 'absconded' by some means or another, according to the workhouse records.

It would seem likely, and quite extraordinary, that its original design allowed for all inhabitants, whether staff or inmates, to enter by the front door as marked on the plan; going down the short corridor the Master's room was on their left (marked 'Board Room') and the door to the dining hall on their right. The Men's Wards on the plan would have been the kitchen, from its position next to the dining hall and the large open fireplace contained in it. Beyond that, on what is postulated to have been the 'barn and skilling', a hospital use is marked, which would have included or been entirely comprised of an infectious ward. On the first floor may have been the workroom, and on the second floor the sleeping accommodation. This space housed nearly 200 people in 1800 and it seems to be almost inconceivable that such a number could have lived in so confined an area. In addition, the Master needed living accommodation; was the room he was allocated all that was supplied? In the 1841 census, his family consisted of a wife and four children, resident with him in the workhouse. Where? By then the rear extensions shown on the 1870 plan had been built and his quarters were in the room adjacent to the Store Room upstairs; but no reference to any further rooms has come to light or can be envisaged. In the earlier period, the first few years of the 19th century, Samuel Gould was the Master and the parish register records the baptism of almost one child of his a year. If they all lived in, no clue as the where or how survives or can be guessed at.

*O.S. 1870*

# Chapter Two

## The early years

So who were the officials in charge of the workhouse; who were the inmates and what did they do?

In answer to the first part of the question, it was the responsibility of the overseers and churchwardens to administer relief, whether 'out-relief' in the applicant's own home, or 'in the House'. Sometimes it is hard to appreciate on what criteria their decisions were made; you would have thought that in a list of 1767 those whose infirmities included being bedridden, lunatic, suffering from fits, cancer victims, blind or lame, would have made ideal in-House material; not so – they were granted out-relief.

The churchwardens at the time the workhouse was first built were John Cook, who was a prominent brewer, and William Footner, of 'Muddiford' (incidentally, from unrelated research proved to be the father of sons intimately involved in an extensive county-wide smuggling enterprise). The Overseers of the Poor were four in number and were: Edward Scott, Stephen Pack, George Verge and Thomas French. Contemporary newspaper references connect Edward Scott with South Bockhampton (Winkton tithing); Stephen Pack was one of a well-represented family of Bure; George Verge came from another local Christchurch family, later associated with brickworks at Hoburne in the parish; a Thomas French occupied Pithouse Farm (Hurn) in 1790. These officials were part of the vestry, a strange organisation in theory consisting of all the parishioners, plus the vicar, overseers and churchwardens; by an Act of 1819 a 'Select Vestry' was created specifically for poor relief policies and included amongst parishioners only the 'principal inhabitants', who at that time consisted of John Spicer, Richard Sleat, George Aldridge, James Jopp, one of the Hicks, one of the Derhams, and one of the Yelfs (the latter of Hurn Farm): all influential, powerful people.

The committee had to oversee the overseers: check all information supplied to the overseers by relief applicants, and to ascertain what property such applicants possessed (or his nearest relations – the purpose being to claw back some of the expenses); to make enquiries about the applicant's normal mode of occupation, what genuine efforts the person had made to find work and whether he had refused any work and why; the number in his family (and whether they were legitimate or not!), their health and occupations; to ascertain details of all strangers entering the parish and advising the overseers about them, especially those likely to become chargeable, and amongst those pregnant women in particular; to keep a list of the unemployed to use for anyone applying to them for labour, and to virtually spy on the relief recipients to advise the overseers of any change in their circumstances.

The role of the overseer was at the same time defined as:

> To receive lists of persons on permanent relief;
> Not to give relief to anyone on that list except in emergencies;
> To inform formally the magistrates every week of all relief given, for their approval or otherwise;
> To collect the rates and draw up the accounts;
> Where an applicant normally received more in wages when in work, any relief given would only be by a loan;
> To read out in church a notice asking those seeking labourers to apply to the overseer for same;
> To print a list of all persons permanently or occasionally relieved, and the amounts paid to them, each year and *fix this list to the church door*!

The overseer or his assistant was furthermore to supply all the goods needed at the workhouse, see that the parish labourers were working conscientiously, and make a report of the conduct of the workhouse inmates for the churchwardens. He was also responsible for relieving wayfarers so long as they were in possession of a pass from a magistrate. Thomas Ruggles, a magistrate in Suffolk writing in 1793, took a very dim view of overseers: they only functioned, he asserted, 'to keep an extraordinary lookout to prevent persons coming to inhabit without a certificate, and to fly to the justices to remove him, and if a man brings a certificate, then to caution all the inhabitants not to let him a farm of £10 a year ... to warn them if they do hire them by the year, then to pick a quarrel with them before the year's end and so get rid of them, rather than [do anything] which shall give them a settlement, ... [and] to move heaven and earth if any dispute happens about a settlement, and in that particular to ... stick at no expense ...'

In 1824 the overseers were Messrs Hannaford, Best, (associated with Iford and Tuckton), Derham, (Mudeford fishing family), and a Thomas Petty who rented a cottage in Bransgore around this time. The churchwardens were John Spicer, the wealthy brewer living at Somerford Grange, and John Hopkins, who rented farmland at Neacroft. It was not always possible to find people willing or able to undertake an overseer's functions; in 1811 James Penleaze(who built the original mansion of High Cliff which preceded Highcliffe Castle) refused to accept the office and was indicted for it. Other officials who took up positions plainly did so to line their own pockets. The level of distress was widespread at the end of the 18th century, and for a short period it was the practice to top up the low wages of labourers with an allowance based on the prevailing price of bread. As the price of wheat rose, the labourers got an amount from the Poor Rate which was calculated in accordance with the size of their family and the price of a quartern loaf (the Speenhamland system). Bread constituted almost two-thirds of the expense of a poor family (Ruggles, 1793). This was much abused – inevitably leading to farmers underpaying their workers in the knowledge the parish would subsidise their wages, and the resulting dependency on the parish demoralised and demotivated the labourers. It was also a wasteful and expensive expedient, albeit well-intentioned.

Vestry records provide some examples of the implementation of the scheme:

April 1795: 'By the unanimous wish, they are ready during the present high price of bread, to grant every reasonable relief to such poor parishioners as shall be found by enquiry to be peaceable, sober and industrious,' (thus attempting to attach a stick to the carrot).

December 1795: a proposal to increase the wages of labourers to 9s a week was approved, 'and that such increases of wages should continue during the present high price of bread and not be reduced until wheat shall be sold at 15s a load'.

Later, the overseers used their personal knowledge of local individuals and their circumstances or character to assist them with their relief decisions.

Thus, a Select Vestry account of their proceedings, in 1824, showed relief dispensed as follows:

Sheets and blankets for a couple expecting a confinement – allowed;
A single man requesting money – allowed;
A petticoat requested – rejected; likewise requests for a shirt and a spade;
Medical relief, wife ill – Dr Quartley to attend;
A house – 'to look out for themselves';
Several people were granted shoes, the commonest request;
A hedging hook – granted;
A window mended – rejected;
A bottle of port wine was granted to the parish surgeon (for medicinal purposes);
Relief – to go and see various named people, such applicants were ordered (it was the duty of ratepayers to provide work for relief applicants, an arrangement known as the 'roundsman system').

One Harriet Tilley requested a spinning wheel. This was also a common request, as it was a means of enabling a widow, which Harriet may well have been, to earn her living without having to come into the House or require parish relief. In this case, the spinning wheel was allowed on condition that she 'returns her old one to this House and teaches no less than six children how to use it' – another means of ensuring the present and future ability of these children to earn a living.

John Pardy asked for a house, but received only the peremptory response: 'To have only this House'. I wonder if this man was perhaps the son of the other John Pardy who warmed the new workhouse with peat back in 1764? Others who applied for relief were also offered only the House, not out-relief. Perhaps they were considered incapable of maintaining themselves independently. A later case recorded one James Saunders '*ordered* into the Poor House'. It may well have been that he was able-bodied, a class of person always treated harshly by the parish authorities. It certainly demonstrates that the overseers selected, by what criteria it is not recorded, who should get assistance and in what form, and who should go without. The Revd Bingley, writing in 1813, had only praise for their sagacity:

> *The affairs of the poor are managed by a committee which meets every Monday morning at the workhouse. They hear the Complaints of the Poor, direct with what necessaries they are to be supplied, and on all occasions act with feeling and liberality. They purchase everything at first hand, and take care that whatever is purchased is good of the kind.'*

One Benjamin Hawes, Esq, at the time had even thought highly enough of the committee to present to them a silver snuff box in 1812: no trace of such a person has been found locally to date.

However, less than twenty years later a different view of the eccentricities of the relief decisions was taken by the Poor Law Commissioners on an inspection in 1832, later quoted.

The daily administration of the workhouse was the responsibility of the Master, appointed by the vestry, and his wife, the Matron or Mistress. At the time there was no training provided for these positions, and the pay was poor, compared, for instance, to the prison service. The quality of recruit sometimes reflected this. One Master, by the name of John Short, features in an extraordinary and somewhat tantalising entry in the Vestry minutes in 1805 in connection with a riot. Astonishingly, the prospect of a riot was taken so seriously that two special constables were sworn in 'to prevent any disorder or riot from being committed', – out of concern for the behaviour of Mr Short during his remaining sojourn at the workhouse, and not out of concern for any outbreak of violence from the inmates. No clue as to the 'repeated

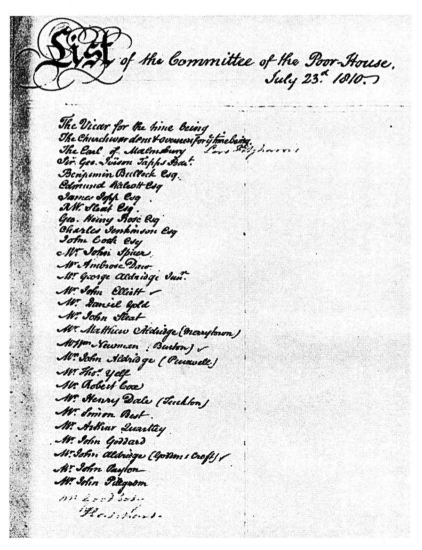

*(DRO)*

23

misconduct' for which he was dismissed is given, but it could be connected with two incidents which were reported in the regional press not long before. In the first of these, one Tabitha Glasbery, at the age of 70, committed suicide by drowning herself in the river rather than face having to enter the workhouse (as was usual in these times, her actions resulted in her body being buried unceremoniously under a public road). Only weeks later, rumours were circulating about 'improper treatment of the poor' at the hands of the churchwardens, overseers and committee, which accused them of denying the poor sufficient food, clothing or accommodation. The rumours were scotched after a vestry enquiry. Mr Short was the Master at the time of these hints of trouble. Of course, in a mixed workhouse such as this one was, another abuse of the trust placed in the Master could and not infrequently did involve the young women and girls; it is difficult and somewhat unfair to speculate further on the actual circumstances, but this period in the story of the workhouse features conflicting evidence, and scanty it is at that.

As before remarked, the position of workhouse master was not in any way prestigious; it appears that the accommodation provided was rudimentary. Public Record Office papers reveal that his quarters were in fact the boardroom when not in use for meetings! According to the memoirs of Benjamin Joy Tucker, the Master's sitting room had a sanded floor, with no carpet or common table, and the chairs had crude rush seats.

Shortly after this incident, a new Master was appointed by the name of Samuel Gould, his wife, Sarah, being the Mistress. He asked the overseers for a piece of carpet and another chair or two, but was brusquely informed: 'No. What you have is quite sufficient.'

Mr Gould must have been a better class of incumbent but after his death in 1813 his wife, Sarah, ruled supreme as Mistress. By 1817, their son, John (born Christchurch 1792), appears in the payments for 'hand cards used in the manufacture' (weaving?) and the following year for 'instructing the children'. By 1824 he had become the Master. He remained the Master until his death in 1864 – a total of 40 years, although his obituary in *The Christchurch Times* erroneously gives 47 years. He is here described as 'an old and much-esteemed inhabitant', having carried out with aplomb this post so 'commonly arduous and difficult', and earned thereby 'the fullest confidence' of the parish officers and the 'respect and esteem' of 'those committed to his charge'. So, who were the people committed to his charge?

A Register of Inmates of 1811 shows that they were of all ages, included entire families and some who were actually born in the workhouse. They left if they died, 'ran off', which several did, including two children – one aged just 13, the other 10, were 'sent out' – incredibly, one of the two people who left for this reason was 90; or sent to the bridewell (one person) or to Salisbury Infirmary.

Many babies were born in the workhouse. It was lawful to commit to prison a repeated offender; the 1824 Vestry Minutes record this as the fate of one Ann Shave, of Ringwood parish, who, 'having lately been delivered of a bastard child in the workhouse' was sent to the magistrates for committal to prison. Most of the workhouse babies were illegitimate. The overseers would make strenuous efforts to seek maintenance from the reputed father in order to avoid having to maintain the child at the expense of the parish (rather as today the Child Support Agency operates). Many original Bastardy Bonds are still kept in the Priory Archives. These were standardised legal documents in which both parents were named, and the father, who had to sign the document, accepted responsibility for the maintenance of his child. An early example from 1773 cites one Mary Vatcher, 'lately delivered of a female bastard child', the father of which, one Christopher Morey, was bound over in the sum of 'thirty pounds of lawful money of Great Britain' to be paid to the overseers and churchwardens.

If a man deserted his wife and family, he was likely to find himself hauled in front of the magistrates. For example, in 1861 a saddler was sentenced to three months' hard labour for this offence. The court took the view that with his trade he was capable of earning enough to support them.

The inmates' occupations in the House at about this time are listed in the surviving records, and included spinning flax and worsted, making and mending clothes, making beads, knitting (probably of stockings, or, by the mid-18th century, gloves), digging the garden, picking hemp, and, of course, the most famous workhouse money-spinner of all, the manufacture of fusee chains. In 1776, a new Master and Mistress had been advertised for (*Salisbury Journal*), specifically familiar with the instruction of flax spinning:

> *WANTED, immediately, an honest, steady MAN and WIFE, who understand Spinning Flax, and will take upon themselves the care of a Master and Mistress, to govern and keep to work the poor in the workhouse at Christchurch, Hampshire. Such persons bringing unexceptional characters with them will be treated with any Monday in the forenoon, by the gentleman of the committee, in the committee-room of the said workhouse. N.B. A man and wife without children will be most agreeable.*

It should be noted that at this time, the occupations were not exactly onerous, with the possible exception of picking hemp, nor punitive, although they were likely to have been tedious and tiring. It should also be borne in mind that at any one time, because of the nature of the population in the workhouse, which would have had a high proportion of the very aged or disabled (not to mention the mentally ill or retarded) and small children, only something like a third to a half of the inmates were actually capable of any work at all.

These occupations helped to subsidise the costs of the keep of the inmates. The employers in the town who took advantage of the system of cheap labour thus provided included William Pickford, William Goff, Charles Chisel and James Mowlem. Children, and 'adults Incapable of severe labour' were put to straw-bonnet making from 1802, working for Robert Millard, who in 1804 was paid the generous sum of £70 to instruct the parish children in the work, only to have £20 clawed back from him in the same year for 'the maintenance and bringing up of the child with which Hannah Cook is now pregnant'!

To return to the fusee chain manufacture, this craft industry was brought to the town by Robert Harvey Cox, a native of Holdenhurst, and within a few years, certainly by 1800, he was using child labour from the workhouse for the manufacture, as well as out-workers in cottages in the area (there were eventually four chain manufacturers locally, the last of which only ceased operations in 1914). According to Allen White, in *The Chain Makers*, it would have been young girls of nine years old or less principally engaged in the intricate processes involved, on account of their nimble fingers. He states that they could have worked for up to 70 hours a week. In retrospect, what appears by the modern scale of values as appalling exploitation was not only in tune with the times in advance of the Factory Acts, but could well have ultimately benefited the children in enabling them to acquire a skill of use to them in the future as adults.

Reference is also made (1819) to a payment to a 'Mr Gouger relative to the children intended to be by him teached in the silk manufactury to Sherborne, £1 17s'.

Later records (1822-32) indicate that weaving was another occupation at that time, probably from wool, an item on a list of supplies from tradesman J Tilley. Leather was still bought in quantity, so shoes must have been made in the House at the time.

*Straw bonnet: fashion plate of 1809 (Ackermann's Repository)*

*Fusee chains and tools
(RHM)*

17th century records held in the Priory Church archives list apprenticeships for the poor children of the parish and their names and those of their employers. In fact, the Poor Law records for Christchurch document these names from 1698 – many decades before there was a workhouse in the town. The documents reveal that the children could be bound to a variety of trades: the Newfoundland fishing trade accounted for some; a range of skills were taught to others. The most unusual on record must surely be mud-wall making. Others in this period include tailoring, cordwaining (shoemaking), husbandry, housewifery and servants, and mariners. Husbandry and housewifery would have been unlikely to be anything more than unpaid drudgery. Alarmingly, after the names of the apprentices in the list 1698-1744 appears the word 'dead' not infrequently.

Some of the girls were put into service via adverts in *The Salisbury Journal* to 'creditable and respectable housekeepers' with a premium of £10 to the employer for each child placed. This was a common practice in those days, and by offloading a pauper at a premium to defray parish expenses, future savings were made, as well as a position found for the workhouse child. The system was widely abused in the parishes generally: girls in service were frequently appallingly overworked.

Our Christchurch overseers thought of another ingenious ruse to reduce the relief expenditure and the level of the Poor Rates. This threat to dispossess those who repeatedly requested relief was issued in 1824:

> *Whereas several persons in this parish receiving constant relief are possessed of cottages, lands and gardens, it is agreed to propose to such poor persons that they convey their respective cottages and lands to this parish, to take effect after the death of such persons, and in the case of the refusal of such paupers to make such conveyances, on account of preserving the same for their children, the relief to those paupers to cease, as it will be expected that they shall be from that time supported by their respective children for whom such cottages and lands are preserved.*

This anticipates uncannily by more than a century the hated 'means test' of the 1930s.

With schemes of this sort, it is hardly surprising to read the observations of the Revd Bingley (MS History of Christchurch, 1813) that 'it is entirely from the excellent regulations adopted and persevered in … that the Poors' rates in the parish of Christchurch are so much lower than those of almost all the other parishes of the county.'

Another practice of the overseers was to hire out workhouse labour on the repair of roads in the parish or farm work. The daily charge was a shilling for an able-bodied man, 10d for someone not able-bodied, and a mere 8d for a man over 60 (Select Vestry minutes 1824). According to the 1832 Poor Law Commissioners' Report, the workmen were permitted to keep one sixth of the wages so earned – a rare and inexplicable departure from standard practice and philosophies. Once again, the hire of labour may have been self-defeating, in that cheaper workhouse labour may have thrown other working men out of a job. An entry in the accounts, proving their use once again, refers to 12s paid in 1820 for the 'Passage Boat to Week [Wick] for the Labourers for working about Potatoes': evidence of labour being used on the land – the passage boat being Wick Ferry or a predecessor.

Herbert Druitt in the *Miscellany* attributed thriftiness to the working man enrolling in Friendly Societies as an insurance against times of want. Bingley, 1813, reports that there were four of these, with a membership of 361. In fact, there were many more: from 1798 there were such societies operating from the George Inn, the Eight Bells, a 'Borough' Friendly Society; and from 1810 the Lamb Friendly Society in Winkton; the Ripley Friendly Society from 1827 which alone in 1848 had 240 members; and so on through the 19th century, with societies at the Dolphin Inn, at Bransgore, and others called the True Britons, Odd Fellowship, Independent Order of Foresters and so on. A procession though the High Street of these societies in 1842 credited membership to 'almost all the artisans and labouring population of this extensive parish', and praised the support which they received from the neighbourhood gentry. With such a membership and system in place, it is surprising that any working man ended up in the workhouse. The town's MP, Sir George Rose, actively promoted savings societies and wrote a tract on Friendly Societies which was influential in raising the profile of these organisations.

Allen White, in *The Chain Makers*, refers to Poor House regulations providing for the children having ten minutes at a time tuition in reading, and all inmates having two hours out of the 24 for air and exercise, although his source is not given. As usual, the boys had better prospects in education than the girls, since the Select Vestry minutes which survive, for 1805 and 1824, record that eight of them could attend St Michael's Loft Grammar School, at the Priory, for free tuition in reading, writing and arithmetic.

Apart from details of occupations, the records can also tell us about other aspects of the inmates' life. They were, for instance, dressed in the earliest days in linsey coats, which material was a rough mixture of linen and wool; dowlas shifts, which were coarse calico undergarments; warper aprons and worsted hose and other clothes made from hessian. Inmates were generally expected to give up such clothes as they had, and to wear special workhouse issue, but the degree of compulsion in Christchurch at the time is not known, although likely to have been obligatory. William Tucker (reminiscences, *The Christchurch Times*) describes the men as wearing clothing, shoes and stockings made by the inmates, the Master having cut out the clothes and shoes himself. Furthermore, a surplus of clothing made in the House was issued to the needy labouring poor outside (Poor Law Commissioners' Report, op.cit). As to the diet, provisions ordered in 1768, the first year that such records survive for, list beef, milk, rice, pork, peas, flour, suet, cheese, butter, beer, molasses and bread (which was to be 'best seconds' – another understandable economy measure). The beer may seem unexpected: in 1835 the Master was authorised to buy beer for himself, his family, and 'such cases in the House as may require it'. Food was weighed, men receiving a slightly greater allowance than women, and children less than women. The illustration on page 29 is of the dietary at the Sopley workhouse in 1825. Its tediousness and paltriness seem pitiful, and they surely must have been, but this period was a time of severe agricultural distress, and those outside such an institution would not be guaranteed to fare any better – especially after the Enclosure Acts.

As to how many people were in the House at any one time, numbers greatly fluctuated. Nationally, the annual cost of all forms of poor relief rose between 1776 to 1785 by 41%, of which 25% was spent on legal expenses regarding settlement arguments. This situation was reflected locally: from a 1768 intake of 62 persons, four years later there were 98, and 125 in 1788. The highest figure reached was in 1800, when it was 171, which declined steadily to under 100 throughout 1803. These figures relate to the original area of the workhouse, before the cottages adjacent were added to the accommodation, and represent a staggering density of people crammed into that space, bearing in mind also that the rear extensions comprising the present costume gallery etc, formerly partly ward accommodation, did not then exist. Thomas Ruggles, writing in 1793, referring to a 'vast increase of the poor's rate', went on to make the accusation that: 'While a tenth part of your countryman enjoy the comforts or revel in the luxuries of life, the patient and industrious

# A Table.

Shewing the names and ages of persons for whom the Master has apply'd to the Committee, for any sort of apparel, specifying the several sorts, with the size and price of each garment, &c and the times when order'd and when deliver'd.

| Names | Ages | Garments &c | Materials | Sizes | When order'd | When deliver'd | Price |
|---|---|---|---|---|---|---|---|
| Ann Sax | 87 | Pair White Hose | Worsted | 5 ounces | 1765 January | 18 Jany | 0 - 1 - 9 |
| William Clark | 51 | Shirt | Canvis | | D° | 8 Jany | 3 - 3 |
| Elizabeth Lawrence | 27 | Petty-coat | Linsey | | D° | 10 | 5 - 0 |
| Ann Sutton | 70 | Pair Shoes & Apron | Roper | | Jany 10 | 15 | 3 - 6 |
| Frances Loor | 17 | Pair Hose Apron | Yarn Roper | 5½ | Jany 15 | 18 | 1 - 5 |
| Thomas Barnes | 13 | Pair Hose | Yarn | 7½ | | 24 | 1 - 5 |
| Mary Dean | 6 | Pair Hose | Worsted | 4¼ | Jany 22 | 29 | 1 - 5 |
| Mary Wimbleton | 27 | Gown Lindsed | Camblet | | | 24 | 1 - 3 |
| Christopher Vincent | 82 | Check Cap | | | | 26 | 7 |
| John Collens | 80 | D° | | | | 22 Jany | 7 |
| Sarah Hurdle | 6 | Shoes | | | | 26 | 2 - 0 |
| Mary Wimbleton | 27 | D° | | | Feb 4 | | 3 - 6 |
| Charles Payne | 13 | D° | | | | 9 Feb | 3 - 6 |
| Elizabeth Parkins | 42 | Hose | Yarn | 8 - 0 | | 6 Feb | 1 - 4 |
| Hannah Dukes | 13 | Jacket & Coat Stockings Apron Shoes | Linsey Yarn Roper | 6 ounces | | | 7 - 2, 1 - 0, 5 - 2 |
| Mary Jay | 23 | Under Coat | Linsey | | Feb 11 | 16 Feb | 1 - 2 |
| Ann Hurdle | 13 | Pair Hose | Yarn | 6 | | | 8 |
| Pint oyl for Shoes | | | | | | 14 Feb | 9 |
| Ann Jay | 1½ | Pair Hose | Worsted | | | | 3 - 6 |
| Mary Gibbs | 49 | D° Shoes | Shoes | | | 20 | 2 - 0 |
| Henry King | 8 | Breeches | Leather | | Feb 18 | | 0 - 7 |
| Eliz. Barnes | 50 | Worsted Stockings | | 2 a | | | 3 |
| Mary Gibbs | 49 | Swath for Leg | Flannen | | March | | 1 - 0 |
| Sarah Coffin | 66 | Apron | Roper | | D° | 12 march | 6 - 8 |
| Mary Denn | 6 | a Jacket & Coat | Linsey | 6 years | | 15 | 5 - 4 |
| James Bowdige | 4½ | Cloathed Coat & Leather | | 4½ | | | 9 - 6 |
| Charles Payne | 13 | Breeches | out of old | 4½ | 11 | 16 | 2 - 9 |
| James Bowdridge | 4½ | Cloathed | Linsey | | | | 2 - 4 |
| Mary Gibbs | 49 | Shift | Dowles | 49 | | | 2 - 4 |
| Mary Scott | 13 | D° | D° | 13 | | | 3 - 6 |
| Mary French | 17 | D° | D° | 17 | 18 | | 1 - 2 |
| John Dean | 12 | Pair Shoes | | 12 | D° | 19 | 2 - 6 |
| Martha French | 17 | Pair Hose | Yarn | 17 | D° | 21 | 0 - 10 |
| Mary Tally | 13 | Shift Apron | Dowles Roper | 13 | D° | 25 | 2 - 6 |
| Mary Jay | 23 | Shoes | | 23 | D° | | 1 - 6 |
| John Dan | 12 | Hat & Hose | | 8 oun | 15 | | 2 - 8 |
| Elizabeth Barnes | 50 | A Shift | Dowles | 2½ ells | D° 27 | | |
| **Total** | | | | | | £ | |

*Table of clothing ordered for the inmates 1765 (DRO)*

multitude are sinking beneath a load of wretchedness and poverty ... myriads have fallen by the sword, disease and famine, the victims of war, led on to their destruction by wretches who have disgraced the human race.' Strong words from an entrenched member of the establishment. From his personal experience as a magistrate, he described conditions for the poor at this time, people whose very occupation as labourers subjected them to acute illnesses, chronic disorders, old age and decrepitude; he refers to the 'depth of wretchedness in the cottages of the poor ... the fascinating charms of intoxication; the consequential habits, idleness and dissipation; the indolence which is concomitant with a broken spirit, and that carelessness or indifference to what may happen in future which is too apt to arise in the mind that cannot see its way through present difficulties.'

Certainly, other records of the year of the highest intake, 1800, shed some light on the causes: sickness was prevalent, we are told in the records: John Short was paid a gratuity of seven guineas in 1802 'for his great care and trouble in looking after the poor in the House during the sickness in the spring of 1801'; the parish register for 1801 records that: 'a general inoculation for the small pox took place throughout the parish which Disorder carried off Forty persons. After the Small Pox a malignant Fever broke out in the Poor House which carried off about Twenty more poor Creatures.' Again, Mr [Phillip] Druitt, the parish doctor, was paid a sum in acknowledgement of 'the extraordinary trouble' he took in 'attending the poor during the above sickness' [of spring, 1801]. By contrast, the vestry meeting was told that at the time of their question, 1868, that there were only 38 people, although the reasons for this will become apparent later, with the account of the changes arising from the 1834 'New Poor Law'. By this time, however, the Victorian economy

*Sopley workhouse dietary, c.1825 (HRO)*

was thriving, the industrial revolution which led to it but which rendered the skills of so many working people redundant, having long passed out of memory.

To accommodate such increases, the parish authorities gradually acquired adjacent cottages. The remarkable photograph below is the only one to have turned up to record all these lost buildings, and is dated September 1861. First to be purchased was one adjoining the workhouse, bought in 1801 for £69. This is behind the dark mass of trees to the immediate right of the workhouse, marked in the 1870 plan as 'kitchens'. John Pillgrem was paid for carpenter's work and thatch on a building 'adjoining the workhouse', in 1803 – presumably, on this structure. Note the vicarage behind before the Victorian frontage was added. In 1814 a pair of cottages – the two adjoining thatched roofs indicate these – was acquired; and the 'Net House' to the right was the final purchase in 1869 at which time the Guardians were being relentlessly pressed by the Poor Law Board, as we shall see, to provide better accommodation. The schoolroom of c.1835 can be seen peaking above the extension at the rear of the workhouse, and the boys' dayroom at the rear of it. Note the edge of a hayrick on Pitts Deep. The only trace that these buildings ever existed is on the end wall of the museum, where can be seen a bricked-in communicating doorway.

The Net House must have been a curious building, the only known record of which is a sale advertisement in 1856 of its contents, the building itself being described as the Stores'. That it was aptly named the Net House is indicated by the items for purchase, which include a flat-bottom boat, a variety of 'Capital Boat Sails and Boat Spars', boat-poles, rush-hooks (for collecting reeds for thatching?), net-trucks, net-corks and lines, part of a mackerel net, something mysteriously described as a net-spreader, along with miscellaneous agricultural oddments such as a turnip-cutter and wagon shafts. One may deduce it was a sort of boat chandlery or the stock-in-trade of a fishing concern.

An intriguing suggestion hinting at the Net House being a structure of some antiquity is contained in a manuscript by one John Mellor in 1872, who connects it to the monastery. Describing the vicinity of the church, he observes:

*The workhouse in 1861, photographed by Henry Castleman from across the river at Wick (RHM)*

*Just across the roadway . . . is a lane called poor house lane where stands the Union or workhouse
. . . a mere row of rather tall whitewashed cottages and at the east end a sort of dilapidated old brick
barn which it is not improbable may possibly at one time have been the Poor Pilgrims or wayfarers
lodgings under the care of the Monks . . . After Prayers. . . they were well wrapped in sacks . . . and
sent to sleep in the great long loft above on a good straw bed, the loft being open to the rafters there
was plenty of fresh air.*

Thus, in a passing reference made by a visitor, important new information comes to light, helping to reconstruct the appearance of these vanished early buildings later absorbed into the workhouse accommodation.

Sometimes the parish agreed to pay people to emigrate – they must have made a well-informed calculation about long-term financial savings to be gained; by these means, Henry Emberley and his family, for example, got to America in 1831, and George Hopkins, a sawyer, his wife and six children were assisted with making a similar fresh start in Australia in 1839 by the provision of outfits and the train fare to London.

An unusual medical incident was recorded in 1827, when Medical Officers Mr Quartley and Mr Goddard were paid £4 4s 'for attending the wife of Henry Cuthbert in an extraordinary case of Child Birth: – This Woman being a vagrant taken in labour in the Street – it was necessary for her to be removed into the Work-House and have this extraordinary attendance, Mr Cave [?] the parish surgeon not then being at home.'

This account brings the workhouse story more or less up to 1834, the date of the upheaval in the philosophy of the workhouse principle contained in the Poor Law Amendment Act which had such far-reaching effects. We find the town described at this time thus: 'The houses had a weather-worn tinge, dripping eaves and moss-grown tiles, if not thatch, coverings. Shops were few and of little account,' (*The Christchurch Times*, 1860: memories of a correspondent, 'well-wisher'). The Tithe Map of 1844 below shows how the workhouse buildings and their surroundings looked around this time.

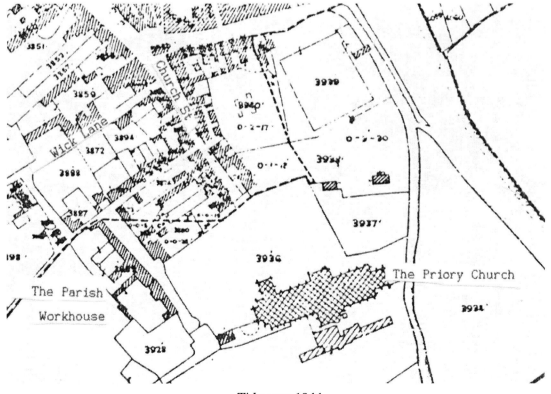

*Tithe map 1844*

# Chapter Three

## Later years

The reasons for the implementation of this Act, which had enormous repercussions for the way in which workhouses were run, and which is responsible for the revulsion which the word 'workhouse' evokes today, were complex.

There was no doubt that the existing provision was being abused, at great cost to the ratepayers, by so-called paupers living the 'life of Riley' at the parish's expense – or so it was thought – or by intimidating overseers to obtain relief (although intimidation was a two-way process). The numbers of relief recipients had escalated dramatically: by 1832 about one in ten people was on some form of relief. This was not entirely, by all means, caused by the system being misused – it was a time of great social unrest and deprivation caused by the industrial revolution, with the advent of mechanisation throwing people out of work everywhere and putting an end to the old cottage industries. Only two years earlier, the 'Swing' riots had spread through the south of England, concentrating especially on the counties of Wiltshire, Hampshire and Dorset, as an expression of the desperation of the agricultural labourers brought about by the advent of threshing machines, the last straw after the disasters of enclosures, with the consequential Game Laws which took away the traditional right to an important means of supplementing their diet; the shortages and high prices occasioned by the protracted Napoleonic wars; the Corn Laws which almost literally took the bread from their mouths, and the impossibility of seeking a livelihood elsewhere on account of the settlement laws. To seek to improve matters by joining forces to press for better conditions caused the culprits to fall foul of the Combination Laws, an example of which will forever be commemorated by the Dorset case of the 'Tolpuddle Martyrs'. There was simply no way to win any sort of livelihood by lawful means. The riots got only as close to Christchurch as Somerley, near Ringwood, at which news the outraged gentry of the neighbourhood galloped off with some fervour to put down the mini-rebellion. The defeat of the rioters crushed the spirit of the aggrieved labourers, and the insurrection was treated more harshly in Hampshire than in any other county involved. At a Special Assizes in Winchester, many involved were transported and some were hung; the Chairman of the Jury was Christchurch's Sir George Henry Rose. Probably never again did the desperate straits of the mass of the agricultural populace reach so dire a point.

The alarming episode created a sudden flurry of anxious attempts to improve the lot of the labouring man in the town, when almost every member of the landed gentry met in the church and agreed on measures to be adopted, such as finding permanent employment for the poor and supplying them with winter fuel and even some cheap land to cultivate. The Vestry even resolved to pay 'those in the parish employ an adequate remuneration for their labour, rather than a limited allowance for their subsistence'. Had it not been for the twin blessings derived from the geographical position of Christchurch, no doubt the violence and destitution would have been as grim here as elsewhere in the county. From its location on the coast, a smuggling industry had arisen which almost certainly involved most of the population of the region in some way, to their undoubted benefit, no matter what occasional and reprehensible incidents of violence it gave rise to: it was bread in mouths. Furthermore, the importance of Mudeford as a 'watering place' has not in previous accounts of the town been fully appreciated, nor the scale of it and the impact on the local economy fully realised. Every season, from about 1790 until at least the 1840s, the village of Mudeford swarmed with aristocracy, gentry and nobility, bringing with them enormous wealth which was not only dissipated in extravagant living, balls at the King's Arms, concerts and so on, but also filtered down to the downtrodden masses (those still awake after the night's energetic exertions on the beaches with casks) through the requirements for servants, provisions etc, and by charitable expenditure. Time and time again it is reported how subscriptions were raised to meet one calamity after another – the effects of a severe winter, or flooding.

It was these visitors who also helped to set up a soup society in the town in 1800 – the year when the workhouse had its greatest number of inmates.

Despite these obvious signs of distress, the threat they presented only served to spur the authorities on to a thorough reform of the Poor Law, whereby the numbers of relief recipients could be drastically cut by the simple expedient of making workhouses adopt a standard of living lower than even the lowliest labourer in work could achieve. In view of the foregoing, that standard was to be absolutely abysmal. No matter that it would give rise to a 'catch-all' situation, and that the apparently scrounging labourers would be affected by the new merciless regime in exactly the same way as would the orphans, widows, cripples and other unfortunates. The aim of the workhouse reformers to distinguish between the 'deserving' and 'undeserving' poor would never entirely be resolved.

Before the new legislation was enacted, each parish was visited by a Poor Law Commissioner; one Captain Pringle duly arrived in the town in 1832 and his report merely commented that Christchurch workhouse was 'clean' – a state of affairs as commendable as it was unusual. However, as regards the principles of relief payment being pursued, the captain remarked:

> . . . a woman, who stated her age to be 59, who was admitted to be hard-working and respectable, and to have only then got into difficulties from her age, was refused assistance as she owned her cottage. On the case being strongly urged, however, by the mayor, who happened to be present [probably Arthur Quartley, as the parish surgeon], one shilling per week was ordered, for which she expressed her gratitude.'

The standard rate in the county overall for the old and infirm, such as this lady, was said by Captain Pringle to be from 1s to 3s weekly. Bearing in mind that pauper labourers were being paid that amount as a day rate, the level of support for this woman was pitiful; it also provides an example of the ruling adopted by the vestry in 1824, referred to in the previous chapter. The captain contrasted this case with that of an able-bodied man 'of about 30, who had four children and 1s 6d weekly,' and who said he had not the money to pay his rent; the parish officers as a matter of policy did not pay rent, but ordered him 10s relief extra as casual. And another, an active sailor lad of 18, who said his ship was at Lymington, and would not sail for a fortnight, received 5s.' Damningly, Captain Pringle's findings overall were that: '... whilst the vestry liberally awarded the cloth and shoes made in the house to farm labourers, the aged and impotent were granted such pittances, that they were dependent on private charity'.

These words echo the mysterious charges made in 1801 regarding the withholding of support from the relief applicants, described earlier. The report's findings also noted that the diet in the workhouses was better than that of labourers outside supporting themselves, and that the children were better clothed, educated and fed than their equivalents in the community at large. Nevertheless, because of their close association with 'bad characters in the House' and the indolence which all being provided for them apparently induced, at least half of the children 'did not turn out well'. Captain Pringle made particularly astute observations regarding the Speenhamland system of paying the labourers partly from the Poor Rates: it suited the local farmers since it kept their workforce within the parish and therefore at their command when the need arose. These very farmers constituted the majority of the vestry and overseers, so the subsidies from the rates suited them very well indeed.

The existing system was obviously shown to have serious inadequacies and opportunities for unfairness to say the least, if not outright corruption, although the remedy was so drastic as to be a cure worse than the disease.

With the passing of the resultant revolutionary Poor Law Amendment Act of 1834, economies of scale were achieved by the creations of 'Unions'. Christchurch was required to join one, quite against the wishes of the vestry, who at a meeting at the end of that year passed a resolution that:

> having taken into consideration the question of the Union of the parish of Christchurch with Holdenhurst and Sopley, we beg to state that the Parish officers of Holdenhurst and Sopley having expressed their opinion that such Union will not be acceptable to their respective Parishes, and

*having also taken the opinion of the rate payers of Christchurch as to the advantage likely to result from that Union, that it was the unanimous opinion that such Union should not take place. They therefore humbly hope, they may not be forced to adopt such Union.*

Forced they were, though, and the Christchurch Union was declared 28 July 1835. The first Board of Guardians comprised: James Taylor (Chairman), John Aldridge, Stephen Groves, Peter Derham, Joseph Hannaford, Joseph Cooper, James Grey and George Olive Aldridge (Vice-chairman). Henry Pain was the clerk and Joseph Scott the Relieving Officer (about more of whom later). John Gould was the Master and Henry Humby the auditor. Henry Pain filled the post as clerk to the Guardians for 27 years and was succeeded by his son of the same name, after his death in 1858.

*G O Aldridge*

New principles were applied: the 'workhouse test' being the one with the most impact, in that those who quailed at the prospect of entering the austere environment of the restyled workhouse had failed the test and were denied relief. The intention of the new Act was to force all able-bodied applicants into the House, but this was never completely achieved, and out-relief continued in some cases as before. Within the House, drab workhouse dress, hard and monotonous 'task' work was enforced, food was rationed and meagre, and the system of 'classification', was introduced – in theory, at least. The old mixed workhouse gave way to a system of division of the sexes and ages, leading to the separation of family members. Furthermore, if the chief breadwinner applied for relief and was ordered into the House, the entire family had to accompany him, and leave when he [she] did. Unfortunately, the new policy of deterrence inflicted its cruellest effects on the most helpless and blameless inmates, as previously remarked upon.

Christchurch parish in 1836 had a population of 7,089 [Poor Law Report 1836] encompassing the tithings of the Borough, Street (Purewell), Bure, Hinton, Burton, Winkton, Hurn, Iford, Tuckton and Wick. Holdenhurst, with Muscliff, Muckleshell and Throop, being already attached to the parish as a chapelry, became part of the Union – thus the future Bournemouth, which eventually swallowed up not only Holdenhurst but Tuckton and Wick, and Iford, came into the equation initially as a sparsely-populated area, but the growth of which had enormous consequences for the future of the Union, as will be seen. Sopley was the other addition; both these additional villages previously had poorhouses of their own.

The new Unions were governed by a Board of Guardians, elected members largely from the farming classes as before; Christchurch Union began with nine. The minutes of 1836 reveal that Ringwood and Burley had sought to join the Union but this did not proceed. Had it done so, we might have seen in Christchurch the construction of a grim new workhouse fortress, such as were springing up all over the country by order of the Poor Law Commissioners. Why the Christchurch parish officers were even more loath to include Ringwood in the proposed Union than they were with Holdenhurst and Sopley is unclear, but it appears that the poverty of that town made them fear a vast increase in expenditure and hence of Poor Rates.

Soon after the Union was created, by express order of the Commissioners, an enlargement was effected at a cost of £350; this consisted of the rear projection from the dining hall (at present containing the Romney Green exhibition) for 36 more people to be accommodated in 18 more beds in two rows; measurements indicate that a space of just over two feet was left between the rows. In fact, the curious widening of this room from the party wall with the original building was made specifically to permit the requisite number of beds to

# E.—Election of Guardians of the Poor.

## CHRISTCHURCH UNION.

**I,** HENRY PAIN, Clerk to the Guardians of the Poor of the CHRISTCHURCH Union, with reference to the ensuing Election of Guardians of the Poor for the several Parishes in the said Union, do hereby give Notice:—

1.—That the number of Guardians for the Poor to be elected for the Parishes in the said Union, is as follows :—

| | |
|---|---|
| CHRISTCHURCH - - - - - - - - | 6 Guardians. |
| HOLDENHURST - - - - - - - | 1 ,, |
| SOPLEY - - - - - - - - - | 2 ,, |

2.—That any person not otherwise disqualified by law who shall be rated to the Poor-rate in any parish in the Union, in respect of hereditaments of the annual rental of TWENTY-FIVE POUNDS, is qualified to be nominated for the Office of Guardian at the said Election, by any person then qualified to vote.

3.—That any Ratepayer who shall have been rated to the Poor-rate in any parish in the Union for the whole year immediately preceding his voting, and shall have paid the Rates made and assessed on him for the relief of the poor for one whole year, as well as those due from him at the time of voting, except those which have been made or become due within six months immediately preceding such voting; and that every Owner of rateable property situated within the said parish, who shall have given to the Overseers thereof, before the First day of February, the statement in writing required by law, will be entitled, according to the provisions of the 7 & 8 Vict. c. 101, sect. 14, to have the number and proportion of votes at the Election of the Guardians for the said parish, according to the following scale :—

| | |
|---|---|
| If the property in respect of which he is entitled to vote be rated upon a rateable value of less than £50 | He shall have one vote. |
| If such rateable value amount to £50 and be less than £100 - - - | He shall have two votes. |
| If it amount to £100 and be less than £150 - - - - - | He shall have three votes. |
| If it amount to £150 and be less than £200 - - - - - | He shall have four votes. |
| If it amount to £200 and be less than £250 - - - - - | He shall have five votes. |
| If it amount to or exceed £250 - - - - - - | He shall have six votes. |

Any Owner of such property who has made such statement may, by writing under his hand, appoint any person to vote as his proxy, but such proxy must, fourteen days previously to the day on which he shall claim to vote, give to one of the Overseers of such parish, a statement in writing, of his own name and address, and also the name and address of the Owner appointing him such proxy, and a description of the property as proxy to the Owner whereof he claims to vote, and also the original or an attested copy of the writing appointing him such proxy.

4.—Nominations of Guardians must be made according to the form below, which is the form prescribed by the Poor Law Commissioners. Such Nominations must be sent, on or before the TWENTY-SIXTH day of MARCH instant, to me,

Who alone are authorized to receive the same. Nominations sent after that day, or sent to any other person, will be invalid.

5.—That I shall, if more than the above-mentioned number of Guardians be nominated for any parish, cause Voting Papers to be delivered on the Fifth day of APRIL next, at the address in such Parish of each Ratepayer, Owner, and Proxy, qualified to vote; and that on the EIGHTH day of APRIL next, I shall cause such Voting Papers to be collected.

6.—That on the NINTH day of APRIL next, I shall attend at the Board Room of the Union Workhouse, at the hour of TEN o'clock in the FORENOON, and that I shall on that day, and if necessary the following days, proceed to ascertain the number of Votes given for each Candidate.

7.—That any person put in nomination for the office of Guardian may at any time during the proceedings in the Election, tender to me in writing his refusal to serve the office, and the Election, so far as regards that person, will be no further proceeded with.

---

*Form of Nomination Paper.*

Parish of _____ }
CHRISTCHURCH UNION. } This _____ Day of _____ 184

| Names of Persons nominated to be Guardians. | Residence of the Persons nominated. | Quality or Calling of Persons nominated. |
|---|---|---|
| | | |

I, being*———duly qualified to Vote in the Parish of———,Nominate the above to be Guardian (or Guardians) for the said Parish.

Signature }
Address } of Nominator.

* Note.—Only one person is empowered to sign this paper, and after the word *being* must insert (*a ratepayer*) or (*owner of property*) according to his qualification.

---

Given under my hand this Tenth day of March, 184

### HENRY PAIN,
Clerk to the Guardians of the Poor of the Christchurch Union.

*Guardians' election form 1840s: note property qualification allocating votes according to wealth*
*(DRO RHM collection)*

*(The Salisbury and Winchester Journal, 1836)*

be fitted in. Above this room was the Master's office, or even domestic quarters, so designed that he could supervise both the male and female yards from the windows (now the curator's office, so no change there!) and also via a glass door keep a beady eye open on new arrivals coming through the entrance door. It is likely that the schoolroom which extended beyond this new construction was added at the same time. Other improvements included the repair of the 'cells' with a new floor; and new brick floor to the Weaving Shop – both revealing new aspects of the interior arrangements.

The First Poor Law Report provides a useful and detailed insight into the new regime in the Christchurch Union workhouse. Tabulated for easier reference these details are:

Admission: either by order of the Board of Guardians, by provisional order from an Overseers of the Poor or a churchwarden or the Relieving Officer. If the case was urgent, the Master was empowered to allow admittance.

Once admitted, the pauper went to a probationary ward to be examined by the Medical Officer. If the person was sick, he/she was assigned to the sick or lunatic ward. The next procedure was to be cleansed, clothed in workhouse dress, and their own clothes purified and restored to them on departure.

Men were deemed to be youths over 13 and women to be girls over 16.

Married couples were permitted to stay together, subject to the approval of the Poor Law Commissioners.

Mothers were permitted to see their children at reasonable times. [No mention of fathers' rights.]

The day was organised by the ringing of a bell and at the start of the day a register of inmates was called.

Children were to receive three hours' tuition a day in the three 'Rs', plus religious instruction.

The diet was regulated carefully so as not to exceed that of the local able-bodied labourers.

Inmates were free to leave after giving three hours' notice, but no able-bodied person could leave without taking out any family with him/her.

No visits were permitted unless the Master allowed it.

Sundays were not to be used for work – except for domestic work! On this day divine service had to be attended compulsorily.

Discipline: for disobeying rules, making a noise when silence had been ordered, using profane language, insulting other inmates, refusing to wash or to work, pretending to be sick, wasting work materials or food, damaging Union property, disobeying the Master – all comprised 'disorderly' behaviour punishable by being confined in a special room, dressed in distinguishing clothes, or put on a punishment diet [usually bread and water]. Worse offences, such as drunkenness or indecency, were classed as 'refractory' and the offender would be confined for 24 hours.

Officials were to include apart from the Master and Matron, a chaplain, Medical Officer, and porter.

It seems that other harsh measures were implemented with gusto: 'ordered the several bastard children marked off in the relief list to be ordered into the Poor House – of a class whose fathers had not paid for their support' (1837 Guardians' minutes).

The next year's report of 1836 includes a preliminary assessment of the effects of the change, contributed by the Union clerk, Henry Pain. He advised the Commissioners that matters in Holdenhurst parish had improved particularly: 'not only from a decrease in the Poor rate, but in the improvement in the morals of the labouring classes, arising no doubt from the fact of their having obtained employment during the winter, and which has operated in some degree to a diminution of able-bodied pauperism'. The Guardians (PRO) were of the opinion that 'there is now a great desire amongst the paupers to procure employment.' So, the objectives appeared then to have been on course; note the absence of all appreciation at this period of any connection between unemployment and unavailability of work – able-bodied people out of work were quite simply malingerers. Mr Pain went on to pay tribute, by special request of the Guardians, to one of the genuine philanthropists in the neighbourhood, Sir G W T Gervis, who, true to style and in an example of many acts of selfless generosity to the underprivileged in his lifetime, took on labourers on his Hinton estate during the winter to save them from having to apply for relief.

The savings from these upheavals were assessed as about 10% – somewhat paltry, it would appear.

A later report, of 1840, provides information on the legal and other costs of implementing the settlement laws which so preoccupied parish officers: of less than £2,000 spent on all relief, £220 went to the lawyers. At around 10%, this is a substantial reduction on the 25% estimated expenditure half a century earlier. That year the Master decided to select several 'paupers for the purpose of dressing them alike for parochial distinction': presumably, to tell at once who was from which parish in the Union, for reasons which are unclear but of curiosity value.

| | | Breakfast | | | Dinner | | | | Supper | | ✱ |
|---|---|---|---|---|---|---|---|---|---|---|---|
| | | Bread | Cheese | Gruel | Cooked Meat | Potatoes | Soup | Boiled Rice ✱ | Bread | Cheese | Bread |
| | | oz | oz | Pints | oz | lb | Pints | Pints | oz | oz | oz |
| Sunday | Men | 7 | 2 | — | 4½ | 1 | — | 1 lb to each with ½ oz of Sugar | 6 | 1¾ | — |
| | Women | 6 | 2 | — | 4½ | 1 | — | | 5 | 1¾ | — |
| Monday | Men | 7 | — | 1½ | — | — | — | 1 lb to each with ½ oz of Sugar | 6 | 1¾ | — |
| | Women | 6 | — | 1½ | — | — | — | | 5 | 1¾ | — |
| Tuesday | Men | 7 | — | 1½ | — | — | 1½ | ditto | 6 | 1¾ | 5 |
| | Women | 6 | — | 1½ | — | — | 1½ | ditto | 5 | 1¾ | 4 |
| Wednesday | Men | 7 | — | 1½ | 4½ | 1 | — | — | 6 | 1¾ | — |
| | Women | 6 | — | 1½ | 4½ | 1 | — | — | 5 | 1¾ | — |
| Thursday | Men | 7 | — | 1½ | — | — | 1½ | ditto | 6 | 1¾ | 5 |
| | Women | 6 | — | 1½ | — | — | 1½ | ditto | 5 | 1¾ | 4 |
| Friday | Men | 7 | — | 1½ | 4½ | 1 | — | — | 6 | 1¾ | — |
| | Women | 6 | — | 1½ | 4½ | 1 | — | — | 5 | 1¾ | — |
| Saturday | Men | 7 | — | 1½ | — | — | 1½ | ditto | 6 | 1¾ | 5 |
| | Women | 6 | — | 1½ | — | — | 1½ | ditto | 5 | 1¾ | 4 |

*Dietary 1836 (PRO)*

It is sometimes hard for us to appreciate from this distance in time just what depths of destitution people could sink to. *The Salisbury and Winchester Journal* comes to our aid once again with an appalling case from nearby Salisbury.

*Destitution.*—On Thursday evening, a young woman was found in a state of insensibility on the steps of a house in Castle-street, her garments, which were very slight, being completely saturated by the rain that had fallen heavily for some hours previously, and which still continued to descend most pitilessly on the head of the unsheltered wanderer. Through the kindness of some neighbours, she was removed to an adjoining house, and every effort was made to restore suspended animation, but for a considerable time without success. A surgeon having been sent for, the Messrs. Winzar were promptly in attendance, who, together with the parish officer, directed her to be taken to the poor-house, where every attention was paid to her during the night, but she still remains in a precarious state. The poor girl, who was evidently in the last stage of destitution, being without money or clothes beyond the scanty habiliments in which she appeared, stated her name to be Jenkins, and that she had that day walked from Frome, a distance of nearly thirty miles.

*(The Salisbury and Winchester Journal, 1840)*

The creation of the Boards of Guardians, of course, took away local autonomy to a great extent, and invested the powers in a national body, the Poor Law Commission. This was replaced by the Poor Law Board in 1847, after the scandal at Andover workhouse in which through the mendacity and corruption of the Master, the inmates, who were on one of the vilest of task-work, pulverising bones, were in such an advanced state of starvation that they fought each other for the marrow.

As instructed at the outset, the first Christchurch Board of Guardians appointed two visitors from their number to report on the state of the workhouse, which practice had in fact been undertaken previously by the overseers as far back as 1815. The classification scheme expected of them never seemed entirely to materialise, although in the 1845 a reference appears in the Guardians' minutes to an additional building to separate the boys from the old and infirm men, which rather implies that since the new Act came into force they had not been so separated. This building, as before stated, is the one constructed at the end of the schoolroom, currently one of the museum offices (approached via the costume gallery). 'Certain additions, alterations and repairs' are alluded to in 1866. Further evidence of a slow progress towards classification is more clearly mentioned soon after, as the Poor Law Board began to harangue the Guardians on this point and about the disrepair of the House. There were seven main classes of inmates: the infirm males, infirm females, able-bodied males, able-bodied females, boys over 7 and under 16, girls over 7 and under 16, and children under 7. By the time the Poor Law Board was making these persistent complaints, the numbers of inmates were regularly below 40 or so, which made it all the more ludicrous that such pressure should have been applied. It also suggests that the intention of the new Act was being fulfilled, and paupers preferred to die of starvation outside than go in – but improved economic conditions played a part, too.

*(The Salisbury and Winchester Journal, 1836)*

CHRISTCHURCH UNION.

THE GUARDIANS of this UNION are willing to receive TENDERS from MEDICAL GENTLEMEN, stating at what Rate they will CONTRACT for the MEDICAL RELIEF of the UNION for One Year, from the 25th day of March, 1836, as follows:—

All cases of Sickness, Surgery, and Vaccination, including Medicines, which may be necessary for all Paupers within the Union, whether belonging to the same, or otherwise.

All Pauper Midwifery Cases, within one mile of the Town Hall, Christchurch, at per case.

All Pauper Midwifery Cases within the Union, occurring at a greater distance than the above, at per case.

No Midwifery Case to be attended without an Order from the Relieving Officer; and the Medical Officer will be required to make a Weekly Return of all Cases to the Board of Guardians, and attend their Meetings when required to do so.

Sealed Tenders, addressed to the Guardians, to be delivered, free of expense, at the Union Board Room, Christchurch, by or before two o'clock in the afternoon of the 7th day of March next.

At the same time and place the Guardians will receive sealed Tenders from persons desirous of CONTRACTING for supplying the under-mentioned ARTICLES, for Three Months, from the 25th day of March next:—

Best seconds Flour, at per sack.
Best seconds Bread, at per gallon.
Good Household Cheese (not exceeding ten to the cwt.), at per cwt.
Good Salt Butter, at per pound.
Good boiling Peas, at per bushel.
Good Soup Beef, at per pound.
Good Rice, at per pound.
Best hard yellow Soap, at per dozen.
Good Store Candles, at per dozen.
Best Coals, at per ton.

Samples of Flour, Bread, Cheese, Peas, and Rice will be required, and the Bread to be delivered at such places within the Union, and at such times, as the Relieving Officer may direct.

The Guardians do not pledge themselves to accept the lowest Tender.

Security to be given, if required.

HENRY PAIN,
Clerk to the Board of Guardians.

CHRISTCHURCH, Feb. 22, 1836. [6074

The Board of Guardians met weekly on Mondays in the office of their clerk, Henry Pain, at the workhouse, in the boardroom shown on the 1870 plan. Over the ensuing years, as the population, especially that of the mushrooming new town of Bournemouth ('Holdenhurst') grew, more Guardians were needed. In 1868 Holdenhurst got another Guardian; in 1871 a further one was elected, bringing the representation of Holdenhurst to four, and the following year Christchurch gained a seventh Guardian. When the Board of Guardians was abolished in 1930, there were over 30 members, so great had been the growth in population. The photograph depicts the Board in 1870 clustered around a flimsy-looking table, spread out with ledgers and other papers, quill pens and ink bottles.

*The Board of Guardians, 1870, in the men's yard. George Olive Aldridge extreme left.*

Whilst the workhouse had room for the paupers, eventually the boardroom could not accommodate all these Guardians, and their meetings in later years were held at James Druitt's house in the High Street, now, of course, the public library.

Other well-known local names who served on the Board were Edward Sleat Elliot of Castle Street, merchant; James Taylor of Winkton, yeoman; John Taylor of Bockhampton, also yeoman; Richard Dale of Tuckton; William Budden of Hurn; William Baker of Bure Farm; Benjamin Baker of Bargates, maltster; John Abbott of Bridge Street, auctioneer; Charles Hicks (also a churchwarden); James Druitt (later the clerk); John Edward Holloway (who founded the Hengistbury Mining Company which operation nearly blasted the peninsula out of the sea); Mr Cooper-Dean of Littledown House; James Aldridge of Throop, mealman, representing Holdenhurst; representing Sopley at one time were William Tice of Sopley Park, a JP and major landowner; and Thomas Henry Tuck of Avon, 'yeoman and estate agent' (PRO), an enterprising man who in 1851 attempted to start a flax industry at his Avon farm but was thwarted when the mill burnt down two years later. *Ex-officio* members were also on the Board for many years, e.g. General Stuart and Lord Malmesbury. All these people were well-known names in the annals of local history.

The first Visitors' Report on the House was disappointing as far as future historians are concerned, containing nothing more remarkable than the observation that 'the attic bedroom ceiling be taken down and the bedroom be ceiled to the rafters'. Perhaps the roof height was too low. An early report from the Poor Law Commissioners is more revealing, commenting as it did on the fact that: 'Nothing has been done for the improvement of the defective Union House since my last visit, but a Committee has been appointed to carry out certain schemes next spring [1847]. The Union is a small one, and there are but few inmates in the workhouse. The manufacture of cloth has been suspended ...' (calling to mind the reference to the Weaving Shop in 1835).

Inmates may have been troublesome on occasions, but so were paid officials. The chief miscreant in this respect was a Relieving Officer, Joseph Scott, who was shown in 1844 to have falsified the accounts: at least £133 was missing, he having recorded payments made to tradesmen that were not made. His exposure only came after several cases of complaint which reached the ears of the Guardians via one of the Medical Officers, Mr Shorto. The case which was his undoing was his attendance on the young female victim of a vicious assault, which was valiantly taken up by Sir George Henry Rose, of Sandhills. The assault followed on the conviction of the attacker for a previous assault on the woman; Sir George was one of the sentencing magistrates. Mr Scott felt it appropriate to threaten the seriously ill woman with an order sending her back to her parish of settlement (Yeovil), charged her with 'unchasteness', and otherwise behaved to her in a 'barbarous and inhumane manner'. This Mary Bishop was not the only case he was guilty of, being so apparently unsuited for the job of a Relieving Officer – many more came to light. He had already been warned by Sir George, after it was found that he was ordering extra food at the parish's expense for the sick instead of paying for medicines as he should have done, to cease to 'pour gall into the cup of poverty which was bitter enough already'. After it was discovered how many tradesmen he had swindled, he was sacked, and Samuel Bemister, at the age of 26, previously a gunsmith and bell-hanger, succeeded him. Mr Scott was, in addition to his post with the Union, also treasurer and manager to the Wilts and Dorset Bank in the town: an embezzler on a huge scale, it would seem. It appears that he hurriedly left the country to avoid justice.

George Whiffen in 1856 was found to have expropriated the substantial sum, for those days, of £210 10s 9d. He admitted having appropriated the Poor Rate funds and was convicted. He was duly dispatched to the lock-up in Bargates (in Spicer Street in the Pit Site, now demolished) whilst a distress warrant was issued against him in an attempt to recover some of the amount missing; but it was in vain, as he seems to have been possessed only of a couch and a small bedstead to the value of £1 12s 6d. Even that paltry sum was reduced to 10s after auctioneer's expenses were deducted. Mr Whiffen was sentenced to three months' imprisonment at Winchester's 'House of Correction'; to the regret of the magistrates this was the most severe sentence they could inflict. An entry in *The Poole Herald* in 1849 records the destruction by fire of the premises of one Mr Whiffen, boot and shoemaker, in the town – perhaps the incidents are in some way related. Mr Whiffen was not the first criminal employee – the case of John Short, the Master, is recounted above.

After the death of the Master, John Gould, in 1864, his assistant, Harry Heath, and his wife Mary, were appointed at the salary of £20 p.a. plus rations. Although there were three other candidates, all with experience in the post in other unions, and Mr Heath had only been an assistant for three months, he was selected. The lack of experience is also demonstrated in that he was previously a draper's assistant – such was the situation regarding qualifications and experience as a workhouse master. However, he had, reported *The Christchurch Times*, discharged his duties to the satisfaction of the house surgeon, the visitors, and the Revd Nash, curate and chaplain. More significantly, he was married to the daughter of John Gould. Whilst he was there, Mr Heath whiled away his time building boats in the loft of the building known as the 'Net House', which was adjacent to the existing workhouse buildings on the church side, and which the Guardians purchased in 1869.

The 'greatly respected' Heaths went on to Sheffield Workhouse, presumably to advance their careers, in 1871. 'Their gentle manners towards all brought into contact with them from without, combined with kindness and necessary firmness to those under their charge, bind on them the esteem of the neighbourhood they leave and the grateful respect of the inmates they tended with almost parental care,' waffled *The Christchurch Times*. Whether this was merely diplomatic or sincere we have no means of telling.

After they left, the Guardians appointed a couple by the name of William and Eliza Clarke, both schoolteachers, formerly of Amersham, he 26 and his wife 38 years old, having no children, at the salary of £40 p.a. and £25 respectively, plus rations (including 10½ pints of beer for him and 7 pints for her!). There is a visiting card in an Admission book which still survives, inscribed with the name, 'Mrs W Sydenham Clarke, Melbury Lodge, Wimborne', which, if it does belong to the same people, indicates that the position of workhouse master was coming up in the world. Michael and Laura Saunderson were the holders of the posts from 1876.

# Chapter Four

# Workhouse life

There survives from this post-New Poor Law period a little pamphlet detailing the inmates for the half- year ending Lady Day (25 March) 1857. The statistics contained therein reveal some inklings of the inhabitants. 91 people were then in the House. The majority, 65, were from Christchurch, with little Sopley supplying 16 – a reflection of the level of rural poverty so prevalent. From neighbouring Holdenhurst only six people are represented, despite the fact that this was now well established as Bournemouth. The remaining four people are described as 'irremoveable poor', which means that they were not from the Union but had gained settlement through having lived in the Union the required five years.

The booklet analyses the reasons for their admission: 18 were infirm, four out of work (therefore, presumably, able-bodied); four people had a father out of work, three of whom were from the shared surname member of one family; two had a father ill, and one had a husband also ill. So the rest of the document lists social calamities of one sort or another as the cause of their misfortunes: 14 children were possessed of a mother whose 'misconduct' was responsible for their plight (prostitution? illegitimacy? crime?); a further three children's mother had deserted them; four children had been deserted by their father. This group tells its own story – four children in one family in the workhouse were deserted by the father, and the mother was also in the House on account of her husband's 'misconduct' (prison?). These family tragedies were supplemented by a mixed group of misfits, chiefly represented by eight inmates admitted for 'misconduct', about whom it is notable that they were all female. One of them, Eliza Pack, aged 29, had been 95 days in the workhouse on account of her misconduct, together with her five children. As the last one was stated to be aged three months, it may have been born in the workhouse. Three further children were orphans. Five 'idiots', one insane (also guilty of misconduct), one 'out of place' (another settlement, category, probably awaiting removal to their parish of origin), and a further four who were ill, examples of the role of the workhouse as a place of treatment for the sick. This role is further corroborated by a newspaper account for the same year, of the tragic case of a terrible accident at the Hengistbury Mining Company works. One of the workmen sustained such a serious head injury from a blasting operation that his brain was protruding from his skull. Still conscious, he was removed from Hengistbury Head and taken to the workhouse. Provision for such cases was rudimentary, and in 1850 a report by the Poor Law Board (PRO) noted its insufficiency, comprising as it did two rooms adjacent to the receiving wards for infectious cases.

To complete the statistics, one vagrant is listed. Perhaps the penalties for sleeping out in the open were not at that time in force, or the beadles appointed to prevent such people entering the town had proved effective. Vestry records from before the Unionisation had agreed to appoint two such beadles to patrol the town's perimeter to this end – 'strolling persons' were also to be discouraged. Certainly, it was the policy seldom to admit able-bodied vagrants. All the same, it had become necessary to have a ward set aside for vagrants in 1844, and the next year a total of 55 vagrants, nine of them females, had been relieved in the Union. Four years later the town was reported to be 'much infested with great numbers of Irish Vagrants; within the last six days 170 have been relieved at our Union, besides a number who demanded but did not receive relief' (*Poole Herald*), no doubt a direct consequence of the railway construction. At this time, they were given a night's shelter only, no food or work because of the lack of facilities. By 1861, so great was the increase in their numbers and 'the many insults the Master had received' (PRO) from them that a Police Constable, James Hornigold, was stationed at the workhouse to search the vagrants before admission. This also had the effect of reducing the numbers, or so the Guardians anticipated, as other unions had adopted this plan of action which discouraged many applicants from this class who were wanted by the law. The illustration comes from *Punch*, 1863; although not concerning the Christchurch Union, the alternative scheme

## ICED VAGRANTS.

"WHAT is to be done with our vagrants?" This was the question, according to the *Dewsbury Reporter*, proposed to the Dewsbury Board of Guardians at a late meeting of that benevolent body, by their chairman, W. CROWTHER, ESQ., who thus proceeded to solve the problem which he had mooted :—

"The CHAIRMAN. What is to be done with our vagrants? They average now 180 or 190 per week, and we must take some steps to reduce the number if we can. The fact is, these vagrants are getting to be a public nuisance. MR. FARNALL told us some years ago, that wherever the plan of washing them had been introduced, the number of vagrants attending was reduced to a minimum. The board took up the question, and two persons were appointed to conduct the affair. The vagrants were washed, fed, put to bed, and in the morning were sent away. I think we can't do better than have this plan again, and if any cash is found upon them, they must be made to pay for their board and lodging."

Let us suppose that the vagrants contemplated by MR. CROWTHER are offenders under the Vagrant Act; rogues and vagabonds; and then we shall be enabled duly to relish the lively and humorous discussion which ensued, whereof portions follow. The Chairman's suggestion was first embodied in a formal motion by a philanthropist :—

"MR. GOLDTHORP. I move that we have that plan, and that vagrants be washed all over.

"MR. WILSON. I second the motion. In the absence of a better system, I support the scheme.

"MR. GOLDTHORP. We have a place where it could be done, and there's plenty of cold water.

"MR. HARROP. Could not the vagrants be made to pump instead, as labour?

"MR. SENIOR. I think you shouldn't carry it out as a punishment, still it is highly necessary that they are kept clean. (*A laugh.*)"

Against the stern but salutary proposal of MR. GOLDTHORP, a political economist doubtless worth his weight in gold, a protest was raised, happily in vain, for it evidently proceeded from a benevolence which must be considered morbid, that is, of course in relation to criminals :—

"MR. J. TAYLOR. I should like MR. GOLDTHORP to blend a little humanity with his proposal. Some of the people may be suffering from weakness, and they ought not to be washed all over, as you propose, unless tepid water is used.

"MR. GOLDTHORP. I have no objection to allow those who don't want to be washed, to be washed twice. (*Laughter.*) It's no use unless as a punishment.

"THE CHAIRMAN. No, no, it's a test—(*a laugh*)—and if you want vagrants kept away there is nothing like washing.

"MR. WM. TAYLOR. Oh, wash them by all means. (*Laughter.*)

"THE CHAIRMAN. When the vagrants are naked, there will be the better chance of seeing whether they are ailing or not. If they are not fit to be washed, a surgeon may be sent for."

The sentimentalist was overborne by the weight of opinions, the lightness of whose expression, however, is quite charming. He thus persisted with his mild but obstinate argument, so pleasantly refuted :—

"MR. J. TAYLOR. The board know very well that no surgeon could be called in. It is just possible that men and women, sooner than submit themselves to such treatment, at this inclement season, will refrain from coming to the vagrant wards, and lie at night in barns, and under hedges. Such a test as this involves cruelty, and I shall strongly oppose the motion.

"THE CHAIRMAN. I wash myself all over each morning, and I find the greatest benefit from the practice, and why not the vagrants?

"MR. J. TAYLOR. I take a shower-bath every morning, and feel greatly benefited, but if I had begun to use it at Christmas, instead of at a more favourable season, it would have made me ill, and it will be the case with the vagrants, if you carry out the plan.

"MR. W. TAYLOR. I think it would produce reaction. (*Loud Laughter.*)"

But the more tender-hearted TAYLOR was not to be put down. The debate continued :—

"MR. J. TAYLOR. There is much in what Old JACK used to quote—'The tender mercies of the wicked are cruel.'

"MR. SENIOR. You don't mean plunging into cold water?

"MR. WILSON. No, only washing and scrubbing.

"MR. GOLDTHORP. I mean washing from head to heel. We shall promote cleanliness, and if they have any money, we can take it for their lodgings.

"MR. HARROP. The water ought to be a little warm, especially at a season like this.

"MR. GOLDTHORP. If the water was not found to be of a proper temperature when they were being washed, I recommend adding some ice, and make it a little colder."

MR. GOLDTHORP'S idea of giving vagrants a cold reception is an excellent one, if, as MR. PEARSON, who is master of the penal institution over which the Dewsbury Guardians preside, said "vagrants chiefly are pickpockets, ticket-of-leave men, and the most lawless part of creation;" and if they are committed under the Vagrant Act. Those conditions being presumed, the sequel of this facetious deliberation will be applauded :—

"MR. PEARSON said he approved of the plan; something obnoxious must be tried or they could not keep the vagrants away.

"The CHAIRMAN. I don't believe that washing is obnoxious; it is as a test we wish to introduce it.

"MR. J. TAYLOR. It looks very cruel, I think.

"The motion was then put and carried; MR. J. TAYLOR being the only person who voted against it. MR. KELLEY was not present during the discussion.

"MR. PEARSON was next authorised to engage a couple of men to perform the washing, and also empowered to get the necessary appliances."

But stop! If the benevolent MR. TAYLOR was right in thinking that

*From Punch's Almanack for 1863*

under consideration by the Dewsbury Guardians, loaded as the account is with sarcasm, demonstrates the age-old difficulty under which the officials laboured, and to which a final paragraph alludes: the impossibility of being fair to both 'deserving' and undeserving' cases, by which the former suffer the penalties designed for the latter. The Christchurch Guardians attempted to distinguish between vagrants and 'wayfarers', presumably the latter being regarded as genuinely seeking work, by allowing the wayfarers an additional midday meal of bread and cheese and no taskwork requirement, but the Local Government Board forbade them to pursue this policy (PRO documents for 1872).

Later statistics show that, in one week in 1880, there were between two and six vagrants in Christchurch workhouse. They were hardly encouraged, their food allowance by then consisting of half a pound of bread at night and the same in the morning. Work was later arranged for the vagrants – the standard oakum-picking taskwork being referred to by 1871 – and protests that became a common feature of the vagrants' wards in the new workhouse were already in evidence in the old: a tramp who refused to do any work and then tore up his clothes was sentenced to seven weeks in jail for his intransigence, in 1878.

It was frequently the case that children, especially babies, were abandoned at the workhouse door. An advert appeared in 1873 in *The Christchurch Times* offering a £10 reward for information leading to the conviction of the person who deposited one such baby at the House – a boy of around 18 months in age.

A large proportion of the inmates had been there, according to this 1857 record, for the entire period of 182 days, indicating that there were many long-stay cases.

The same informative pamphlet lists the current Guardians: W W Farr (nicknamed by Benjamin Joy Tucker 'Old Far and Near'), George Aldridge, Edward Sleat Elliott, James Taylor, Richard Dale, Herbert Plowman, Charles Clarke, Lieut. Col. Simmonds, James Aldridge, Henry Bone and Mr Whitcher. The last two represented Sopley and remained in office many years; Mr Whitcher was a farmer who lived at Throop House. Messrs Simmonds and James Aldridge represented Holdenhurst. Almost all these people were farmers. Another of the Holdenhurst/Bournemouth Guardians was the Revd A M Bennett, described by Mary Graham in her book *The Royal National Hospital* as that town's first vicar, also responsible for the building of many Bournemouth churches, a 'serious, dedicated man'. William Farr lived at the imposing Iford House – long since vanished – and was also a JP.

The parish officers were:

Mr A Q Palmer, Surgeon (salary £70);
Mr R S J Stevens, also Surgeon (salary £70);
Mr H Pain, Clerk to the Guardians (£50);
Mr J Gould, Master (£20);
Miss Sarah Gould, Matron (£20);
Mr S Bemister, Relieving Officer (£70);
Mr H Pain, Clerk to the Overseers (£40);
Miss Gould, Schoolmistress (£32).

The two H Pains, as previously noted, were father and son; the son was in the following year appointed Clerk 'in the room of his late lamented father' (*The Christchurch Times*). He held the post until 1876, when he resigned in favour of James Druitt, who became a Guardian in later years. James Druitt was probably the most powerful figure in the town for many years, not only as a solicitor and JP, but as chairman of almost every conceivable public body, and a major property owner and developer – most of Springbourne and Moordown were built on his initiative and finance, and he owned many houses in the High Street in Christchurch. His son, Herbert Druitt, was entirely selfless, a brilliant antiquarian and local historian, passionate defender of all matters relating to history and heritage, and eventual owner of the workhouse which forms the subject of these first chapters.

Samuel Bemister was another notable Christchurch worthy: seven times mayor of the town, his public service was commemorated by a fountain which gave its name to the town centre Fountain Roundabout and is presently situated at the entrance to Bargates.

The Master, Matron and schoolmistress were granted rations as part of their (meagre) wages: each week, the Master and Matron were entitled to precisely 28lb of bread, $1^1/_2$ lb of butter, $1^1/_2$ lb of sugar, 6oz of tea, 10lb of meat, 8lb of potatoes, 3lb of cheese, three gallons of beer (presumably, between them); and the schoolmistress 6lb of bread, $^1/_4$lb of butter, $^1/_2$ lb of sugar, 10oz of tea, $1^1/_2$ lb of meat, 7lb of potatoes, 3/4lb of cheese and 7 pints of beer.

The document also provides the first mention of the school. On the 1870 plan, it is shown on the site of the present museum's costume gallery, with a yard each side for the boys and girls. Miss Lucinda Gould, another member of a virtual dynasty of Goulds, was appointed schoolmistress in 1843 at the age of 24, a very early date in the era before compulsory education, although the schools were not necessarily renowned for quality of instruction during this period. PRO records reveal that children were formerly cared for by an inmate who had

*James Druitt (RHM)*

then left. Some unions delegated the task of teaching to an inmate, and it was not unusual for the children to be subjected to great cruelty, but there is no evidence for this at Christchurch in this period. Miss Gould was highly thought of by the Poor Law Board, being awarded a Certificate of Competency in the First Division from the Committee of the Council on Education, in 1849, and the school got a good report, but in the end she deteriorated because of her health. Lucinda's sister, Sarah, became the Matron after the death of her mother, Lucretia, in 1856 after four years of paralysis, and another sister, Mary, as previously mentioned, married a subsequent Master, Harry Heath, the pair then taking up these posts after the death of John Gould, her father, in 1864; with the departure of the Heaths in 1871 the Gould era ended after 66 years.

Lucinda Gould died of cancer in 1871; her obituary described her as a 'useful and painstaking public servant'. She had been increasingly ill in the final few years, her children became 'deficient in liveliness' and did not show 'much intelligence' [school inspection, 1869]. Her replacement was a Miss Caroline Nunn, though she resigned after a year, succeeded by a Miss Martha James, who stayed two years, then a Miss Clara Langley, who lasted a mere eight months, after which a Miss Emily Hales followed. She was given a report of 'satisfactory performance' by a Poor Law Board school inspector in 1877. Three years later she quarrelled with another member of the school staff, who deemed herself 'ill-used' by the lady. Few reliable conclusions can be drawn from all this, but the illustration from the 1851 Great Exhibition edition of *Punch* magazine indicates what the enclosed, stifling, unstimulating confines of the workhouse schoolroom could be like for a child.

# THE CINDERELLA OF 1851.

### THE SCHOOL-ROOM.

IN the workhouse school-room, choky and small,
That looks out on the workhouse wall,
Sit the pauper children, drearily,
Under the pauper mistress' rule,
Mumbling, and stumbling, and stuttering wearily,
Over the tasks of the workhouse school;
While the sun-light smites uncheerily
Sodden faces, blank of thinking,
Eyes that cannot keep from blinking,
Little bodies, sore and sinking,
That scarce hold up on bench and stool.

But on the side that's out of the sun,
In the furthest corner, and darkest one,
Two little pauper heads are mingling
Their scanty growth of pauper curls,—
Two little pauper faces tingling,—
Two pair of pauper eyes rain pearls,
As two little hands go slowly singling
The sense, word by word, of those tattered pages,
Hoary and brown with the thumbing of ages.
What is the lesson that so engages
The thoughts of those little pauper girls?

Never, I ween, was so eager look
Fasten'd on Primer or Spelling-book;
No—'tis the school-room's hidden treasure,
Bann'd and banish'd, but loved the more,—
The book of mystery, awe, and pleasure,—
The glorious book of fairy lore,
That charms even pauper childhood's leisure,
With its marvellous tales of dwarf and giant,
Of ladies distraught, and knights defiant,
And a world of wonder that moves compliant
To the waving wand of the fairy corps.

*Punch*

Inspections around this date reveal that there were very few pupils, averaging a mere 14, who (in 1871), whilst passing a 'pretty fair examination', were 'not advanced'. The inspector went on to advise that 'the teacher should endeavour to improve both herself [Miss Nunn] and the children'. The schoolroom was furnished with desks and forms, 'Irish books', maps and blackboard – a typical Victorian classroom is conjured up. The children would generally stay on at school until they obtained their certificates, which took some of them longer than others. Their education comprised Religious Knowledge, Reading, Spelling, Penmanship, Arithmetic, English Grammar, English History, Geography, and something mysteriously entitled 'Industrial Skill' – which was garden work for boys and sewing and knitting for the girls, or washing. Then the girls could be released into service, unless she was clever enough or fortunate enough to be apprenticed as a pupil-teacher to the schoolmistress, as young Charlotte Pearcy was in 1848 (PRO records).

There is some evidence for ill-treatment later on. In 1881, when the children were at Tuckton Farm, as will be described below, a woman by the name of Elizabeth Collis, described as the 'housekeeper of the school of Christchurch Union', appeared before the local magistrates charged with an assault on one Elizabeth Brine, a child at the school. Mrs Collis claimed she was not in the habit of beating children at all, a claim that was met with laughter in the court. She was fined 5s and she and her husband left their employment shortly afterwards. At least this shows that mistreatment was not entirely ignored – just not prevented from taking place.

Workhouse children could actually attend a local National School once these came into existence in the mid-Victorian period, and generally did well as a result of mixing with their uninstitutionalised peer group, but in Christchurch it was to be many more years before the workhouse children enjoyed that advantage. The confinement must have been seriously detrimental to them and engaging staff to teach them was fraught with difficulties. An extract from a Poor Law Board Circular of 1870 puts it thus:

> Suppose a young man after serving an apprenticeship to his profession and passing two years in a training college accepts a charge of a workhouse school: he soon discovers that teaching is the least part of his duties. He has to rise at six o'clock in the morning to see his boys washed before breakfast. He has to attend three times a day in the dining hall, to superintend bathing, combing, scrubbing floors, making beds etc; to take the boys out for exercise and to see them to bed at night. So that if he does his duty conscientiously he is fully engaged from six in the morning till eight at night. This unpleasant course of duty goes on day after day without intermission or change. Saturday is no holiday and Sunday is no day of rest . . .

And the writer goes on to compare this exhausting drudgery with the far superior conditions of service to be obtained in a National School post.

Pauper children were also expected to help around the House, the girls with the women on scrubbing and laundry tasks, the boys helping the men in the garden cultivation (produce, of course, not for floral displays!), despite the reluctance of the Guardians to permit the adults to mix with the children. The 'loose women polluted the minds' of the girls and led to their 'ruination' – a hint that the earlier coy reference to misconduct may in truth have been prostitution. This well-founded concern illustrates the drawbacks to the mixed workhouse system and the reason why the classification – so lacking in this union – was not as vindictive as it might otherwise appear.

A new destiny for the boys is first mentioned in 1875, when the Guardians went off to Southampton to inspect a training ship. After this, a life at sea became a common prospect for workhouse boys for many years to come.

The adults continued to be gainfully employed – those in the minority capable of being so – picking horsehair was a new and tedious task added to the previous list. The diet appears to be similar, but tea and bacon appear on an 1868 dietary, and coffee by 1878. As always, obedience was strictly enforced: one able-bodied man got a pound of potatoes instead of a pound of pudding for refusing to attend church – and then three weeks in jail for refusing to work. Certainly, there were discipline problems aplenty, some of which came to the local magistrates' court and provide insights into the atmosphere of barely suppressed violence that must have characterised the workhouse. Examples from the 1850s court records illustrate the problems of Master John Gould:

> *On Sunday night last … at the normal bedtime, 8 o'clock, all the other women were gone to bed. Edna McGuire did not. I told her to go to bed – she said she wouldn't. She persisted in refusing – I was obliged to force her all the way from the lower part of the garden to her bedroom. She came out again after she was put in her room. She gave no reason. I was obliged to send my daughter to her. On the Monday she asked for her clothes. I told her I should detain her to answer for her misconduct. She ran away.*

Edna's spirited defiance cost her 21 days' hard labour. The case sheds light on 'misconduct': if everyone in the workhouse pamphlet of this date described above with that appellation had committed like offences, the workhouse must have been a very unruly place indeed. Soon afterwards, the harassed Master found one Elizabeth Scott in the yard breaking windows with a stick, something she had threatened to do if Mr Sharp was not sent to her. Mr Sharp was probably Risdon Darracott Sharp, local solicitor, which must have been significant although why is a mystery. The damage of £1 2s plus costs was Elizabeth Scott's punishment, or one month in prison.

One group of inmates not previously mentioned is the frankly named 'lunatics'. These people were from the early days sent to asylums: Fisherton House in Salisbury being one, and the Hampshire County Lunatic Asylum at Knowle, Fareham, being another. In 1857, eight lunatics from Christchurch Union were maintained at Knowle, which opened in 1852. The history of this institution is fascinating in itself, and the subject of a comprehensive study called The Knowle Experience. 'Imbeciles' were in a different category, and remained at the workhouse, William Tucker, in his *Reminiscences of Christchurch and Neighbourhood* (1921), as worded in *The Christchurch Times*, recalls such unfortunates during the time of Master John Gould:

> *The water for the use of the House was dipped up at the quay into a barrel and wheeled to the premises by a half-witted man, whose name was Charley Chissel, and who also blew the bellows for the organist at church. On one occasion, after the service was over, Miss Tullock* [the organist] *said to Charlie: 'Didn't I play well today?' The next Sunday the organist could not play until she told Charlie that it was he who helped her to do so well* [this man was not so stupid as he seemed!]. *The organ at that time was on the Rood Screen* [which it was until 1847] *and I used to sit in a pew with my cousins by the side of it and give Charlie pieces of tallow candle, which he ate.*

Charlie Chissell died in 1850 at the age of 81, having been a workhouse inmate since he was about seven years old. Mr Tucker continues:

> *At the workhouse, in a cell facing south, a lunatic by the name of Jones was chained to a post in the rear; in fine weather the door was kept open and he could be seen crouched on his haunches and singing 'I'm going to London, to London. I'm going to London.'*

> *Knowing one of the sons of the Master, I often went with him to see Jones, and I regret to say we sometimes teased him, but woe betide the person who got within his spring.*

Hugh Jones appears in the 1841 census, aged 60. The reference to a cell is interesting, in that John Pillgrem, who was a skilled carpenter and joiner and built the Barracks and the King's Arms amongst other notable buildings in the town, was paid to build two cells in 1809, and in 1813 there were payments for a chain and harness. The chains could, however, have also been purchased for a weaving process. The 1870 plan shows a square area to the south of the boardroom which could possibly be the cells referred to.

The PRO papers provide a wealth of further information about this poor man. It is not surprising he is remembered as having been crouched, since from medical reports it appears that his legs were contracted from having remained in the same position for years, and his chin actually rested on his knees. He refused to wear anything except a shirt, and a coverlet over his face and shoulders. He had been in the workhouse all of forty years, since 1806, after having been discharged on account of his insanity from the navy, into which he was press-ganged during the French Wars. After wandering about the country he appeared in Christchurch and was recognised as the son of a doctor once in practice here. His habits were 'dirty', but he was harmless unless anyone made the unwise attempt to clothe him; he spoke to no one except, rarely, the Master. For fifteen years he had lived with the other inmates, until his violent tendencies caused him to be put in isolation. The Union clerk assured the Commissioner in Lunacy that Mr Jones did not receive any restraint (despite the eye-witness account above), and was 'very decrepit'. The Assistant Poor Law Commissioner who considered the case recommended his removal to an asylum, but the Guardians claimed no treatment would help him nor would his accommodation be improved on; nevertheless, this ill-clothed man was kept in a room without a fire, and was acknowledged by the Guardians to have 'offensive habits and to be an improper person to occupy the same room as the other inmates'. It was, said the report of a visiting Commissioner, actually unlawful to detain lunatics in a workhouse for more than fourteen days. The Commissioners in Lunacy finally ordered the Guardians to put him into an asylum in 1848.

Were the Guardians attempting to save money by not sending him to an asylum? A table of returns for 1847 shows the number of mentally ill, and that only two of the afflicted were kept in the House, out of 15 – the aforementioned Hugh Jones and Charlie Chissell. It will be seen that their maintenance was 2s 7½d a week, as opposed to the asylum patients costing 12s.

The Hampshire County Lunatic Asylum at Knowle had not then been built but Fisherton had. Even after Knowle opened in 1852 conditions for such people did not improve: over twenty years later a further Lunacy Commissioner's report was scathing about one such sufferer's plight. James Togarth, returned to Christchurch Union on trial, soon went mad again from being confined in a 'gloomy' room, deprived of any occupation, in pain from sciatica brought on by the damp stone floor he was actually sitting on (suggesting not even a chair was provided for him); unsurprisingly, the poor man was threatening suicide.

The County Asylum quickly became full: in 1879, it asked the Guardians to take back their 'harmless' patients, but the reply was that there was no room to do so. The Commissioners in Lunacy produced a report on the Christchurch workhouse after visiting it on its last legs in 1881, and concluded that 'the accommodation is so bad [that it is] not suitable or adequate for any class of the insane [on account of] defective premises'. These poor afflicted people must also have been confined in the same wards as the sane, when not in chains in the cells – a mutually intolerable state of affairs.

| ANNUAL RETURN, 8 & 9 Vict. cap. 126. | | | | | | | | | | | | | |
| --- | --- | --- | --- | --- | --- | --- | --- | --- | --- | --- | --- | --- | --- |
| **PAUPER LUNATICS CHARGEABLE ON THE 1st DAY OF JANUARY, 1847.** | | | | | | | | | | | | | |
| A TRUE LIST of all LUNATICS, and IDIOTS, chargeable to the Parishes comprised within the *Christchurch* Union, in the County of *Southampton* Sex, and Age of each, and whether dangerous or otherwise, and for what length of time they have been supposed to be of Unsound Mind, and where confined, or how otherwise disposed | | | | | | | | | | | | | |
| NAME | Age | Sex | Parish to which chargeable | In a County or Boro' Asylum, and what Asylum, and when sent thither | In a Licensed House, and where, and when sent thither | In the Union Workhouse | In Lodgings, or Boarded out, and where | Residing with Friends and where | Weekly Cost of Maintenance and Clothing | Whether Lunatic or Idiot | Dangerous to himself or others | Of dirty habits | For length... Unsound Mind |
| Charles Chissell | 80 | Male | Christchurch | | | yes | | | 2-7½ | Idiot | not | not | Bir. |
| Hugh Jones | 68 | Male | " | | | yes | | | 2-7½ | Lunatic | not | yes | 40 y. |
| John Croucher | 52 | Male | " | | | | | | 12- | Idiot | yes | not | Bir. |
| William Lizzard | 62 | Male | " | | Fisherton | | | | 12- | Idiot | not | not | Bir. |
| William Browne | | Male | " | | Royton | | | | 12- | Lunatic | yes | not | Bi |
| Betty Hiet | 50 | Female | " | | Oct 29th 184 | | | | 12- | Lunatic | yes | yes | 2 yr. |
| Susannah Berry | | Female | " | | | | | | 12- | Lunatic | yes | not | 3 yr. |
| Ann James | 50 | Male | " | | 4 years since July 16th 1842 | | | | 12- | Lunatic | yes | not | 5 yr. |
| Jane Hatcher | 19 | Female | " | | | | | yes Christchurch | 2- | Idiot | not | not | Bir. |
| Caroline French | 29 | Female | " | | | | | " | 2- | Idiot | not | not | Bir. |
| Mary Farrant | 33 | Female | " | | | | | " | 2- | Idiot | not | not | Bir. |
| Maria Corbin | 20 | Female | " | | | | | " | 2- | Idiot | not | not | Bir. |
| Henry Hopkins | 62 | Male | Sopley | Fisherton Asylum | | | | | 12- | Lunatic | yes | not | score |
| Mary Perkins | | Female | " | Oct 29th 1845 | | | | | 12- | Lunatic | yes | not | Bir. |
| Sarah Barrow | 60 | Female | " | | | | | yes Christchurch | 2- | Idiot | not | not | Bir. |

*(PRO)*

Medical Officers sometimes left a lot to be desired, despite the standing in the annals of local history of the names of Quartley, Goddard, Palmer – as later, with Dr Legate. The worst case involved one Mr James Shorto, MO from 1837, who in 1839 found it too much trouble to ride out to East Parley to visit an elderly man, James Dowling, in agony with bowel pain, which the MO did not consider worthy of a six-mile journey to attend to. He did send some 'powders' via Mr Dowling's son, and later that day, on hearing of the worsening of the symptoms, some other medicine with the recommendation to take castor oil; by the time Mr Dowling was visited it was too late and his death ensued an hour afterwards. Thomas Eyles, of Merritown Farm, alerted the Guardians, and a subsequent investigation by Mr A la Court found the Medical Officer so negligent in his treatment of the pauper, that despite the Guardians' assertion that Dr Shorto exhibited 'kindness and humanity' he was asked to resign and did. Four years later he was quietly reappointed. Mr John Bryer Goddard was appointed in 1840 but did not have the double qualification required (Member of the Royal College of Surgeons, and Licentiate of the Apothecaries Company of London). In 1846, MO Mr Palmer was complained of to the Poor Law Commissioners on account of being unqualified. He was also guilty of signing a medical report that he had delivered babies that in fact had been delivered by another, unappointed, deputy. He was again the subject of complaint three years later for sending out his deputy, James Fitzmaurice, of Bridge House, in his stead with some useless powder to a Throop man in intense pain who died the next day. He transgressed again in 1863, in which year out of 2,269 visits to the sick in the Union 2,113 were made by his deputy. Dr Fitzmaurice became Medical Officer for the Western District (of the Union) and workhouse six years later but promptly resigned within months from his own ill-health. It was at this point that Dr Henry Thomas Harvey Mead was appointed in his place. Yet another well-known Christchurch medical man, Dr William Watmough, of Bridge Villa, was in 1871 found guilty by the Poor Law Board of 'very serious neglect of duty' regarding a smallpox case at Ripley which led to the disease spreading to a further four people. He was seriously cautioned and soon after resigned. He was nevertheless reappointed only two years later after the resignation of Dr Morrill.

A notorious case of abuse arising directly from the settlement laws arose at Fisherton House and concerned a Christchurch woman. Letters held in the Local History Room at Christchurch Library, together with contemporary newspaper accounts, piece together the shocking story. It concerned a young lady, German by birth, who was hired as a servant in 1878 by a lady then staying in Bournemouth (in the Christchurch Union, of course). The new servant was soon found to be insane, and her employer sent her to the asylum, which was then managed by Doctors Finch and Lush. After a few weeks, her employer not unreasonably refused to continue to maintain her ex-employee. On receiving this intelligence, Dr Lush tried without success to persuade the Christchurch Guardians to take her. The Guardians responded that she was the responsibility of Fisherton parish. Two or three weeks later, the young woman was unceremonially dumped by the side of a road in Bournemouth, on the instructions, it was implied, of Dr Lush. She was taken by the police to the Knowle asylum at Fareham, where she was maintained by the Christchurch Guardians whilst the settlement arguments continued. This is a tragic example of the inhumanity of the settlement system and of the resulting treatment of the helpless poor or sick by those who should have looked after their welfare. The Guardians, in an understatement, called the actions of Dr Lush 'highly improper'.

Another asylum, Nazareth House (one of a chain), was frequently used for children, but there were others that were used over the years, for example, the Western Counties Idiot Asylum at Starcross in, Exeter, another in Chichester. The Starcross asylum was established in 1864 specifically for children. Yet that same year, two women, probably inmates, were also recruited 'to assist in the bedrooms occupied by the Idiots'. An idiot was mentally handicapped but a lunatic was mentally ill.

Life had its small pleasures for the incarcerated paupers, from time to time. The most well-known occasion was, of course, Christmas Day, when the Guardians would lay on a traditional meal, the first reference to this being in 1867. On New Year's Day, the borough's MP, Admiral Walcott, treated them to a dinner. One Mr Kerley, of Bournemouth, probably the same person later to become a Bournemouth Guardian, gave the sum of 10s to be spent on nuts and oranges (rare luxuries at the time) for the youngsters, and soup and tobacco for their elders. In 1872, the Clerk to the Guardians, James Druitt, and the wife of Guardian J E Holloway set up a fund to raise money for 'some good cheer' for the inmates. Another benefactor was the Hon. Miss Wrottesley – about whom I have no other information.

**DR. FINCH'S ASYLUM for the INSANE,**
FISHERTON, near SALISBURY, WILTS,
under the immediate Superintendence of the Resident Proprietor, W. C. FINCH, M,D. Senior Physician to the County Hospital, &c. &c.

The above Establishment (conducted for many years by Dr. Finch's Father) has been recently repaired and decorated, and so arranged as to promote to the utmost extent the health, comfort, and convalescence of the patients.

In, and out-door amusements of every description, together with healthful exercises are amply provided.

The Gardens and Pleasure Grounds are extensive, and afford every means for recreation.

The chief object aimed at in this Establishment is not so much the seclusion as the CURE of the Patients.

Cottages within the grounds and in the neighbourhood are secured for the more affluent, as well as horses and carriages.

Attendants and Nurses are always in readiness to take the charge of patients at their own homes.

For Prospectuses, Terms, and Legal Forms, apply to Dr. Finch, Fisherton, near Salisbury.

*(Salisbury and Winchester Journal, 1848)*

The curate, later vicar, of Christchurch, the Revd Z Nash, became a regular benefactor, every year treating the inmates to a tea. In 1880 this consisted of 'ham, bread and butter, plum and seedcake etc', and personal gifts of buns and oranges and 'sundry other gifts'. Particularly appreciated would have been the half pound of tea for each old woman, and doubtless the same appreciation would have been felt by the old men for their gift of tobacco. The Revd Pretyman of Bournemouth was another sincere and generous benefactor, and a Guardian for many years. It would be difficult to over-emphasise the value that the children in particular would have placed on these rare opportunities to leave their dull confinement, where they would have been unlikely to have had any personal possessions, let alone toys, and to mix with a normal family.

There seemed to be usually about 50 to 70 people in the House in the 1850s, but the number dwindled, and in the 1860s was often hovering around 40. *The Salisbury and Winchester Journal* remarked in 1852 that there were so few inmates in the House – just 40 from a Union population of 8,500 – that the Master had to hire outside labour to take the corpses for burials. These pathetic inmates were apparently comprised of all those who could not avoid the new-style workhouse; in the words of Guardian George Aldridge, 'the great majority of inmates are of naturally weak or disordered intellect – of previously immoral life, or of aged persons far advanced in second childhood. Of the children, many inherit vicious tendencies. A Master and Mistress, more kind and gentle than many parents, are taxed to their utmost.' (1867: the Heaths were the unfortunate struggling and harassed officers attempting to keep control of this motley group.) The absence of the able-bodied was partly economic regeneration, but those who had no alternative to the workhouse seemed to experience a softening of attitudes after the rigours of the system immediately following the 1834 Act: 'aged persons' seemed to be positively made welcome. An 1879 boardroom proposal that all those over 70 and living alone 'should have the *privilege* of going into the poorhouse where they could be better looked after' (my italics) received general assent, with no reported raising of disapproving eyebrows.

This improvement in attitudes is borne out by a remark from George Aldridge to a vestry meeting that: 'The Poor Law system has improved of late years, and it was necessary that the morality of the inmates should be looked after in a better way than had formerly been the case.' What he was referring to in part was the need to elevate the minds and principles of the remaining decrepit and dissolute or plain dim-witted inadequates who spent their days no doubt engulfed in tedium and regimentation. Who really knows what it was like in the close confines of the workhouse walls? No one has left a diary to tell us. Only the cases of violent assaults on each other or angry breaking of windows, which periodically enliven the court case reports, give clues as to the realities of such a life. Nevertheless, sometimes those with psychic powers have sensed the traces of former occupants:

> *8 June 1924. B.D.* [Bertie Dear] *went to Red House ... and heard someone singing and went up to Museum and saw a woman sitting on a chair in front of door of Waterford Room, light hair, ringlets over shoulder – gigot sleeves, full skirt, singing from a book. Looked up and then on book again – as he approached she faded away, and as he receded she came back again.* (Diary of Herbert Druitt.)

# Chapter Five

# The end of the old workhouse

1867 and 1868 are the years when the future of the workhouse's present building was weighed in the balance and found wanting, and the date from which the long search for alternative premises began.

The town was a small and inconsequential place at this time: 'Christchurch consists for the most part of one long straggling street with in many places long intervals between the houses,' a letter from the Guardians to the Local Government Board bemoans in 1875. But, Bournemouth, of course, was in a quite different league. In the words of one of the Guardians: 'Forty years ago, Bourne was a mere stream, but now it was as broad as the Thames of London.' The Guardians estimated the housing stock in Bournemouth to be increasing by about 200 houses each year.

As mentioned previously, the predecessor to the Local Government Board, the Poor Law Board, had been reproaching the Guardians about the workhouse for some time. Little details were leaking out to the local press – at this time and until 1877 no reporters were permitted at board meetings. News that the House was condemned by the Poor Law Board as 'inconvenient' was nevertheless reported in 1867, as was the news that the Poor Law Board had threatened the Guardians with an order to build a new workhouse if they did not enlarge the present one. When the Guardians did present a plan for such an enlargement, the Poor Law inspectors insisted on a new one being erected; furthermore, if they did not comply, the Board would force the amalgamation of the Christchurch Union with that of Ringwood. The whole story is revealed in correspondence between the Guardians and the Poor Law Board, whose report described the House as 'dilapidated and badly arranged for classification', the site 'low and confined', the accommodation 'bad and defective' (bearing in mind the range of decrepit cottages it had spread into). The report went on to bemoan that 'the only means for separating the infectious from ordinary sick cases is in different rooms in the body of the workhouse … the ventilation and light are defective. No particular arrangements are made for the recreation of the inmates. The children walk out. There is no paid nurse. The nursing is performed by the inmates …'; this state of affairs, said the Board, could only be remedied by the construction of a new workhouse – something it was to take another fourteen years to achieve. At the very least, separate infectious wards should be provided. It was following these events that the Net House already referred to was purchased – perhaps to supply the wards for infectious cases as urged by the Poor Law Board. Certainly, it was a fact that the existing hospital provision was 'bad', referring to the converted barn structure (PRO documents for 1873).

A vestry meeting to discuss the matter was called – the workhouse building was still owned by the vestry. The Guardians sought to purchase the buildings for themselves. At the meeting, in 1868, it was revealed that the Poor Law inspector had actually condemned the House repeatedly on the grounds of absence or insufficiency of classification, the dilapidated state of the building and the confined site. The Guardians not illogically pointed out that it was absurd to try to classify 40 or so occupants into up to 28 different divisions, and they showed some compassion to the inmates in remarking: 'The present inmates of the House were only like a family. If there were any couples, why not treat them liberally and let them live out of the House?' This revolutionary, anti-New Poor Law idea from the unlikely source of James Druitt must have astonished the inspectors. Contrast this remark with that of George Aldridge at the close of the preceding chapter. In fact, of the 40 inmates, four were old men, 11 old women, seven adult men, five adult women, and 11 children – 43. Mr Druitt also pointed out to the Poor Law Board that the cost of extending the workhouse, some £2,500, would be better spent in providing cottages and gardens for a hundred people. After all these heated altercations between all parties, over many months and even more meetings, the workhouse was sold to the Guardians for £600, on condition that Guardians used 'every means in their power to induce the Poor Law Board to abstain from insisting on any large expenditure on the Union Workhouse' (PRO). The exchanges had become so abusive between Elias Lane and George Aldridge that the latter stood down as a Guardian, and James Druitt, formerly the clerk, took his place.

A report from the Commissioners in Lunacy at the same time supplied further evidence of the state of the House, for it was found by them to be 'entirely unfit for the detention therein of any class of inmate of unsound mind', although it was clean and the patients were kindly treated. Despite such charges, the Guardians were determined not to comply with the Poor Law Board's urgent recommendation to build anew, arguing that the present site could not be bettered for convenience of situation, not least for the Guardians, that it was also 'open and airy', and also healthy – no case of infectious disease having ever arisen in the workhouse, and all cases admitted had 'speedily recovered' without disease spreading. There was also plenty of room (PRO). Further inspections from the Poor Law Board commented on the provision of baths being sufficient, but there were no lavatories, and no mention is made of how such sanitation was provided. The 1870 OS plan shows earth closets in the yards; possibly this was the provision. At this time, all water was still being fetched by hand, and basins in bedrooms or dayrooms used for washing in. An inspection of 1872 pointed out that the men were having to sit around in their dayroom on backless benches stood on the unprotected stone floor; the replacement of the flagstones with floorboards dates from this time, but the room is very small and must have been severely cramped. It was divided into infirm and able-bodied classes – the former having the luxury of the large fireplace still in situ. These two rooms, 17' by 15' 9" and 13' 9", were considered capable of holding 28 men (PRO papers for 1856) – not much legroom.

The following year, the Guardians proposed a radical rebuild on the existing site. In letters to the Poor Law Board, they submitted a scheme to rebuild the cottage portions of the House and construct a new school and laundry on the rear boundary. This did not materialise. By 1871, it was apparent that the Guardians had merely patched up the building to save any further expense to the ratepayers. They were often torn between these two loyalties, but their first duty should have been to the poor. It must have been then, as today, a hard balancing act. An edition of *Punch* for 1860 puts it in a nutshell:

> *The nature of the office discharged by these gentlemen is commonly misunderstood. They are supposed to be guardians of the poor. This is not so. They are no more the guardians of the poor than the Police are guardians of the pickpockets. The Poor-Law Guardians are the guardians of the pockets of the rate-payers against the poor, and their business is to make the poor cost the rate-payers as little as possible.*

Another report from the Poor Law Board in 1871 revealed the Guardians' obstinacy: the House was not only 'unfit' but 'dangerous', and the Guardians had been busy constructing an infectious ward at one end without sanction (it is unclear whether or not this was the newly purchased Net House). The female vagrants were housed in a 'dark and damp' room and it was later revealed that as there was no 'receiving' (reception) ward, new arrivals in this category, and probably all arrivals, were examined by the Medical Officer in the entrance hall, today tastefully occupied by an elegant grandfather clock and framed samplers, by way of contrast.

The Guardians finally acknowledged that on the present site they had no room for further wards, having failed in an attempt to buy further land on the south from the Brander family, and decided to take the opportunity of the Portfield Enclosure being made at that time (enacted 1878) to keep their eyes open for a new site on the common land to be released in consequence. The news in the local paper of this development led to a correspondent not unreasonably writing to enquire why, given that the workhouse once held nearly 200 inmates, room could not now be found for 60. No reply was received, but the need for separating the inmates into the required classifications was undoubtably the reason. It was no longer acceptable to mix the ages, sexes and medical cases as had been the practice for so long.

Amidst the vestry squabbles, another major row was looming, and it led to a Poor Law Enquiry. The Union's Medical Officer, one Dr John Sinclair Morrill, had complained that he was being frustrated by the workhouse officials. The Relieving Officer, Samuel Bemister, responsible for the administration of out-relief, kept altering the doctor's order forms and refused to pay for port he had ordered for his pauper patients, instead substituting Tarragon wine. Dr Morrill was infuriated, claiming that this had led directly to the death of one patient, a TB case, and increased suffering amongst others of his workhouse patients. Mr Bemister had also, said the doctor, asked 'improper' questions in obstetric cases (this sounds most unsavoury). The doctor also accused the clerk, Mr Pain, of delaying his salary payments and vaccination fees, altering figures in his contract regarding additional vaccination fees, and interfering with his orders. The Guardians made counter-accusations of discourteous conduct, failure to reply to letters, and making unfounded complaints.

After hearing the evidence at length from both sides, the inspector found for the Guardians, with the small proviso that Mr Bemister should not have altered the doctor's orders, and invited the doctor's resignation – yet another Medical Officer found wanting.

The belief in the efficacy of alcohol as a medicine seems at odds with current knowledge, but was then quite orthodox. After all, it is a stimulant to the nervous system. One aged lady in the workhouse was prescribed a pint of wine a week for several years. 'It must have been an ineffectual sort of medicine', Guardian Elias Lane dryly remarked.

A turnaround in the numbers situation arose suddenly in the 1870s after the low figures of the previous decades, and did more than any Poor Law inspector to persuade the Guardians of the need for a new workhouse. The Guardians wrote to the Local Government Board in 1878 that the workhouse was full – there were 73 inmates at the beginning of that year and 88 by the end – and not only were they being forced to give out-relief when they otherwise would not (much to the literal relief of the applicants, I suspect) but that they were considering sending the children out of the House to a vacant property owned by a member of the Board. This member was Frederick Moser, who resided at Carbery House in Southbourne, another historic house long since demolished.

It was to his property, Tuckton Farm, that most of the children duly went, with their schoolmistress (see photo/map overleaf). No thought appears to have been given to those children who were thereby separated from one or both parents left in the House, but it must have been a welcome change to be somewhere which was then very much still open countryside – even though they were still cramped and had to sleep two to a bed. Perhaps they slept even more to a bed back at the Union workhouse – who knows!

The firm of Peeks in Iford Lane in Tuckton, in recent years relocated to the Fairmile area in Christchurch, until their move occupied the last of the old farm buildings. The site has been redeveloped with housing. It was at these farm buildings that a certain Mr Rolls assembled the aircraft in which he subsequently died at the ill-fated air show of 1910 at Hengistbury Head.

The Guardians now set about with vigour to find a new site, and much of their time over the next few years was taken up with the extraordinary palaver which accompanied their efforts. Buying the land was one thing; getting the architects to design a new building proved to be quite another. They were now

Christchurch Union, Hants.

Clerk, James Druitt, Solicitor.

Days of Meeting first and third Monday in each Month at 2 p.m. at the Clerk's Office

Christchurch 31 Jany 1878

Dear Sir

In consequence of the crowded state of the Workhouse it will be proposed at the Meeting of the Guardians on the 4th February to hire a house in which may be placed the Children or other of the Inmates

Yours faithfully
James Druitt

feeling the pressure of the population growth: claims on the Union had doubled even within the last few months.

They first of all plumped for a site near the railway line, somewhere in Portfield, but later started to purchase on a piecemeal basis parcels of land at Fairmile on which the new workhouse was eventually built. Some of it was bought from small landowners after suitable haggling: £600 to a Mr E Davis here; £150 to a Mr Budden there. Lord Malmesbury and Sir G Gervis parted with some of their acreage, as did Sir George Meyrick. The Board purchased more than their actual estimated requirements as their original intention was to build in addition an isolation hospital, after selling the surplus land to the Christchurch Sanitary Authority, but this did not materialise (the hospital was eventually constructed in Marsh Lane, but nothing survives of it now, as is so often the case in 'historic' Christchurch). By late in 1877, the land acquisitions had been completed – at least for the initial buildings which went up; as will be seen, much more was later acquired.

*Tuckton Farm*

Messrs Creeke and Burton were appointed architects at the beginning of 1877. Christopher Crabbe Creeke warrants special mention in that not only was he the first surveyor for the town of Bournemouth, and left his trademark curving roads in the town centre to this day, designed the extensions to the Royal Bath Hotel, the Central Pleasure Gardens, the Dean Court estate and other elegant villas, but he was also the second president of the Architects' Association and had designed workhouses elsewhere, including one at Chippenham which is now a listed building. His work at Christchurch workhouse's new site is the only undertaking he accepted in our town, and it is an insult to a man of such stature and talent that his work here now lies in ruins, instead of having received the protection and recognition it so richly deserved. This commission was also probably his last, since he died of throat cancer in 1886. His partner was Edgar Burton, who went on to design many other buildings on the new site after Mr Creeke's death. With this eminent partnership enlisted, everything seemed ready to proceed without any more undue hitches.

But it was not to be.

In May of that year, the Guardians were already expressing their 'extreme dissatisfaction' to the architects for the delay in the completion of their plans. By October, their impatience had increased. In February of the following year, 1878, James Druitt issued the pair with an ultimatum. One or the other of the architects then attended board meetings with their plans, but were infuriatingly unreliable in this, leading Mr Farr to accuse them of being 'either utterly incompetent or thoroughly neglectful'. Eventually, the Guardians decided to dispense with with the architects, but did not carry out this threat; part of the problem was that both Creeke and Burton developed illnesses during the design stage, which further delayed proceedings.

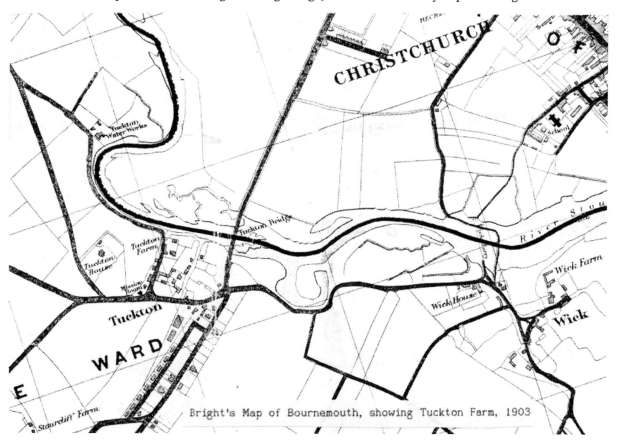

Bright's Map of Bournemouth, showing Tuckton Farm, 1903

The plans proved to be too ambitious. The Local Government Board suggested that the children's wards should be omitted at that stage, on grounds of cost. A scheme for a clock tower above the entrance arch was abandoned, as was the bakery. The infirmary was postponed. When the Guardians chose the lowest tender for the buildings finally approved, from Henry Blachford of Bournemouth, at £11,865, Mr Baldwyn Fleming, the Local Government Board inspector overseeing operations, warned them that Mr Blachford must have made a grave miscalculation. His estimate was £2,000 less than the next nearest one, but the Guardians, as they were often later to do, rejected Mr Baldwin's advice and accepted the tender. The capacity of the new workhouse was finally decided on as 200.

Even when the plans were in front of them, the Guardians could not have looked them over very carefully, as they were full of complaints as the buildings were going up. The vagrants' wards were disgraceful, they said: a zinc roof, open gratings on the floor, no heating – the Guardians expressed themselves 'horror-stricken at the wretchedness with which [the vagrants] had been provided'. There was no provision for fires, the coal hole was 'a ridiculous place', said Mr Holloway (himself an architect amongst other commercial activities), 'only capable of holding about two tons', and he had 'never seen a place so ill-adapted for the purpose required as this was. There were pumps that could never be used at all, all in the wrong places, and with no troughs to them, and many other out-of-the-way things,' he continued. The architect blamed the Clerk of Works for 'irregularities on his certificates for payment, who soon became so ill himself he could no longer supervise the construction, and so on.

The late Mr. Christopher Crabb Creeke.
*The First Surveyor to the Board of Commissioners.*

*(The Bournemouth Visitors Directory, 1890)*

It is possible that all these difficulties arose from the fact that the great boom in workhouse construction had long gone; the Christchurch Guardians were attempting an ambitious scheme nearly fifty years after the New Poor Law era of the 1830s. As a result, the new workhouse design was a radical departure from its predecessors, reflecting attempts to find new solutions to the accommodation requirements. The resulting buildings were therefore most unusual in terms of workhouse layout. Kathryn Morrison, of the Royal Commission on the Historical Monuments of England (now part of English Heritage), having studied the design, described them as having been based on the 'pavilion' principle, of blocks with separate functions linked by corridors, and as such, she advised, unique in the south of England outside of the metropolis (private correspondence). Unfortunately, their rarity did not save them.

Eventually, despite the series of hair-tearing calamities, the new workhouse complex was at last ready and kitted out for the new occupiers. Plain, substantial furniture was chosen, with the usual careful watch on unnecessary expense. A local furniture dealer by the name of W G Spickernell provided an estimate which included 30 iron bedsteads with mattresses and cocoa matting to fit the bedsteads; for the Master and Matron superior items were supplied, including Walton's Patent Linoleum of best quality, a five-frame Brussels carpet, matching Axminster rugs, and Kidder carpets – some improvement there from the sanded floor endured by the first workhouse masters of the 18th century!

The big day arrived on 23 August 1881. The first lucky inmates were able to walk – no doubt heads held high with pride – under the archway entrance in Jumpers Road and take up residence in the wards especially built to segregate the ages and sexes etc, on either side of the impressive quarters for the Master and Matron. They gathered in the dining hall to hear the Chairman of the Board of Guardians, James Kemp Welch, confide in them that 'workhouses are a necessary evil, but in the Christchurch Union everything was done for the comfort of the inmates which a kind Master and Matron could do.' A 'substantial meat tea', reported *The Christchurch Times*, 'was given to the inmates to mark the occasion,' at the Chairman's expense. This included half a pound of tea for the women and a quarter of a pound of tobacco for the men. It must have been quite an expenditure for Mr Kemp Welch – wealthy he may have been, but such generosity over and above the call of duty was typical of the age. Music and readings, no doubt of a suitably elevating nature, ensued.

In reality the Guardians knew that they now had the premises with which they could comply with all the requirements of classification that the Local Government Board had been demanding for so long, and that this would have a profound effect on their relief policy. 'The new workhouse', said the Chairman to the Board, 'offered the greater facility which they would have for encouraging thrift among the poorer classes, by offering the House in many cases where they now granted outdoor relief.' He stated that he would not advocate 'harsh change' in the matter, but 'one should gradually but certainly change the present system, and at all times to treat persons with careful habits differently from those who were more careless.' These words sounded reasonable on the surface but also ominous – 1834 had arrived in Christchurch by 1881.

*James Kemp Welch*

Whilst the building of the new House was being attended to, the Guardians also had to deal with the problem of the existing one. The children were still at Tuckton, although that was so cramped that some had

to remain at the old workhouse, doing virtually nothing as their teacher was with the other children. There was some discussion of adapting the new buildings to accommodate them by dividing up wards, but Inspector Fleming's advice was on this occasion taken – such a scheme would spoil the appearance of the new buildings, scupper the all-important classification plans, and expose the children once again to the 'baneful' influence of the more incorrigible adults. Alternative arrangements had to be made.

Ideas considered included keeping the old House exclusively for the children. This was ruled out as the value of the building and its potential for reducing the debt incurred from the loan was too tempting. Perhaps half of the workhouse could be converted for their use and the other half sold. This too was rejected as impracticable. In the end, the Guardians set about adapting the old empty House for the children and their schoolteacher. Prior to the alterations, Mr Kemp Welch took a look around it and declared that, 'I have never in my lifetime seen a place I was so ashamed of … It is an astonishing thing that it had been occupied for so long.' The outer wings of the decrepit building were closed down, and the area in the middle, corresponding to the approximate area of the present museum, was patched up for the children.

Meanwhile, the Revd Pretyman visited the children at Tuckton in 1880, and expressed himself pleased with their academic attainments. He also exhibited the compassion that some of the Guardians were undoubtably motivated by. Reporting back to the Board, he attempted to persuade them that it was not the fault of the children that they were in the workhouse, and the experience could 'prey on their minds in years to come'. Such revolutionary sentiments did not impress Mr Waterfield, the current chairman, who dismissed such nonsense as unwelcome 'sentimentality'. The workhouse children were, he said, 'paupers after all that was said about them', and he would not accept that they felt any more disgrace than did those children on out-relief.

*The workhouse from the rear at the end of its working life, showing the extent of the dilapidation. In the foreground the long, low range is probably the privies: there was no internal sanitation. (RHM)*

The children returned from the farm in October 1881. The old workhouse was to remain their 'home' again for another five years. Here is what the editor of *The Christchurch Guardian* thought of them:

> *The juvenile paupers of the Christchurch Union may thank their lucky stars that 'the lines have fallen unto them in pleasant places'. There is only one drawback to their perfect bliss. The mansion in which they are domiciled is in a somewhat dilapidated condition . . . the frolicsome young gentlemen seem inclined to let in more air rather than to restrict it; for while the caretaker is engaged in cooking their dinners, they are equally busy in breaking the windows. Had Oliver Twist been fortunate enough to have lived under the bountiful regime of the Christchurch Guardians, he would never have had occasion to shock Mr Bumble's sense of propriety by asking for more. According to the statement of Mr Lander at the [Board] meeting on Monday last, these juveniles fare sumptuously every day, and as they enjoy the utmost liberty, being quite beyond the control of the old man who has charge of them, and by way of amusement indulge in the innocent pastime of breaking windows, we may conclude that on the whole their life is a tolerably happy one, and they are not likely to want to change it. There are Unions where they manage these things differently. Have the Guardians ever tried the boarding out system?*

# Chapter Six

## The Red House

The 'juvenile paupers' finally joined their former fellow-inmates when their accommodation was completed in 1886.

The Guardians then pressed ahead with the sale of their old building, which by then was exceedingly dilapidated. At auction, it was sold to the Revd T H Bush, vicar of the Priory Church. The bidding was hotly contested by others, amongst whom was Samuel Bemister, the Relieving Officer, a Guardian, Henry West Jenkins (also a prominent builder) and, oddly, Mr Blachford, the builder of the new workhouse.

A clue to the sight that the old House must have presented to its new owner is evident in the remark of Guardian Elias Lane after the sale, which was that this would be the right time to ask that the tipping of stone and refuse material against its walls be discontinued. 'It not only looked disgraceful,' he said, 'but considerably narrowed the road near the church.' He did not, he said, like to see the place so neglected as it was in this respect.

The Revd Bush demolished the women's wards, kitchen, and stores, cottages and Net House to the east of the present building, which were apparently about to fall down unaided, having been out of use for five years. In their place, the Revd Bush built the stone wall which now fronts Quay Road. In place of the hospital wing on the other side, which it will be recalled could well have dated back to the beginning of the 18th century or earlier, he built stables, and these are now used as the art gallery. Another section to go was the laundry rear extension, and the school building, on the site of which the vicar built a greenhouse; traces of the whitewash remain today.

So, the present museum building represents approximately half of the original set of buildings, and was renamed by its new owner as the Red House.

The Revd Bush kept the Red House as the family home until his death in 1909. It was then purchased by the Druitt family – in fact, by the widow of James Druitt, Matilda, from whom it was passed down to her son Herbert Druitt previously mentioned as a leading antiquarian and writer on

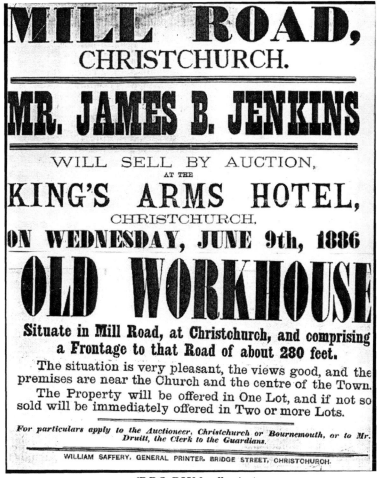

*(DRO RHM collection)*

historical studies, in 1916. His friend H E Miller, a verger at the Priory Church, who was also a keen amateur photographer, lived in the Red House at this period, 1909 until 1920.

During this period, its ultimate role as a museum was anticipated by Herbert Druitt from about 1919 until about 1923, when he would open it by private arrangement to permit examination of his extensive collection of local artefacts, particularly archeological material. But its primary purpose for him was as one of his many stores for his other collections – of books, documents, costume plates, paintings and other works of art, amongst countless other articles of local history interest.

*The former workhouse in 1943: one of Herbert Druitt's stores for local history artefacts*
*(National Monuments Record Centre)*

It was his wish that the Red House should become a permanent museum for the town, but because of the apparent intransigence of the local authority, probably compounded by a mistrust of this complex, increasingly curmudgeonly and outspoken champion of all and everything to do with the town's history – and a fierce and vitriolic opponent of anyone seeming to destroy that heritage – his ambition remained unrealised until his quieter sister, Charlotte, gave the building to the town in 1947 after inheriting it from her brother. The photograph above was taken in the year of Herbert's death, 1943, and clearly shows the difficulties he was experiencing from a hostile populace, mainly of young boys, who were all intent on damaging the structure and content of his treasured storehouse. It is a visible comment on the disparaging attitudes so commonly adopted towards those who fight to keep things of historic importance, which at the time are not recognised as such. Note also that the original workhouse door is the only door; the present second door nearer the archway dates from the museum period. There are no windows on the ground floor at that point, where there are two today, and no long window above the original doorway.

The first task of the trustees of the new museum was to clear the enormous collection: in some parts of the ground floor it was literally holding up the ceiling. No work appeared to have been done on the property for years; the roof leaked, the windows were broken, as stated above, the garden heavily overgrown. Mr Druitt had lived for many of his last years at Woodstock, in Barrack Road. It took three years to get the Red House to a state where it could fulfil Charlotte's legacy and her brother's generous wish, since when this lovely building has become one of our town's greatest assets; a far cry from its humble origins, yet, in its own way, still fulfilling a need for the local populace. But, more than anything, it remains as a memorial to all who for one reason or another had found life too much of a struggle to manage on their own.

# Chapter Seven

# The new workhouse

Back in the sprawling new premises, the Guardians held their first meeting in the new boardroom. This was not where the present one is, but closer to the archway, and the same width as the adjacent single-storey reception range. Whilst there were relatively few Guardians, the accommodation for workhouse business was sufficient.

There was, not unnaturally, a considerable amount of mutual back-slapping at their achievement, and they all seemed to have forgotten the grievances they had expressed whilst the buildings were under construction. 'Every accommodation for the Guardians ... excellent and convenient provision for the press ... remarkable fitness for the purpose for which [the workhouse] had been erected', were just some of the remarks made before they settled down to hear the chairman's speech. 'The old Select Vestry system', he began, 'administered the Poor Law relief, and money was given in lieu of wages. The labourers demanded this as their right and often relief was given out of fear. To alter this state of things the Act of 1834 became a necessity.' He explained that since those days men could not simply desert their families in the knowledge they would get parish relief, as both he and the family would be put in the workhouse. The implication was that the extra space would allow the Guardians to apply these rules much more strictly.

## Early Buildings

The map below shows the original group of buildings that was constructed in the first twenty years of the new workhouse.

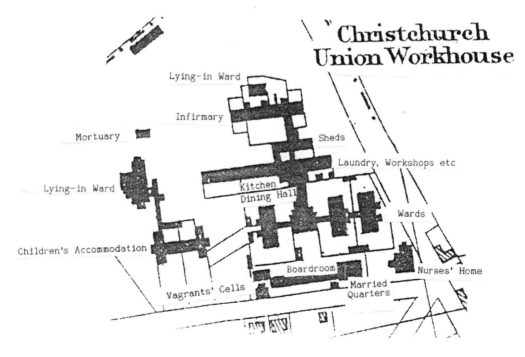

*Bright's Map of Bournemouth, 1903*

In 1881, the components of the group which welcomed the inmates from their former abode are described below.

Above is the archway that all inmates would have entered by, flanked on the left by the lodge of the porter to whom they would have had to report on arrival, and on the right by the boardroom and clerk's office. The boardroom was later rebuilt on the site of the married couples' quarters. The architects had originally designed a clock tower for this entrance, but a previously stated, it was not incorporated on grounds of cost. Note the married quarters provision for two couples.

*Rear of entrance arch with typical Christopher Crabbe Creeke flourish*

*Female vagrants' cells*

The vagrants' cell wards were situated on the extreme left of the entrance range, and were extended substantially on later occasions as the number of vagrants increased with the growth of Bournemouth and because of other social and economic factors (see plan overleaf). The male vagrant ward had six 'cells', with cubicles adjacent in which they had to do the day's 'task' in return for the night's shelter and food, such as it was. The task was stone-breaking, and was exceptionally hard work, deliberately so in accordance with the workhouse policy of deterrence. This facility is omitted from the female ward. The women would have had another task, such as picking oakum. Note the larger cells in this section, which were to accommodate those female tramps who had children with them. The disinfectant stove was for the vagrants' clothing. Note also the baths: it was compulsory to be bathed on admittance. Also shown on the plans (and still remaining until 1999 when the walls and yards were destroyed to create a layby) are the exercise yards, strictly separated for males and females.

The Master's House (p. 69): this graceful house, carefully situated to enable the entrance to be constantly supervised, was the quarters for the Master and Matron. It was designed in the popular Italianate style.

There were three sets of wards, a set on the extreme right having been added in 1895 in identical design to the 1881 original, because of the increased male accommodation needed. At the front the elderly and infirm classes were placed, and the young and able-bodied at the rear. The wards were linked by corridor to the Master and Matron's quarters and through there to the inmates' dining hall beyond.

As this shows, the classification system had the desired effect of separating the able-bodied from the aged, men from women (therefore, husbands from wives; the married quarters were only for certain categories, e.g. the over-60s). The kitchen and stores are at the rear: note the tradesmen's workshops. Of particular interest in this plan is the oakum shed in the yard of the able-bodied men, another example of the deterrence principle. This was tedious work involving separating tarred and tangled rope, often causing painful bleeding fingers.

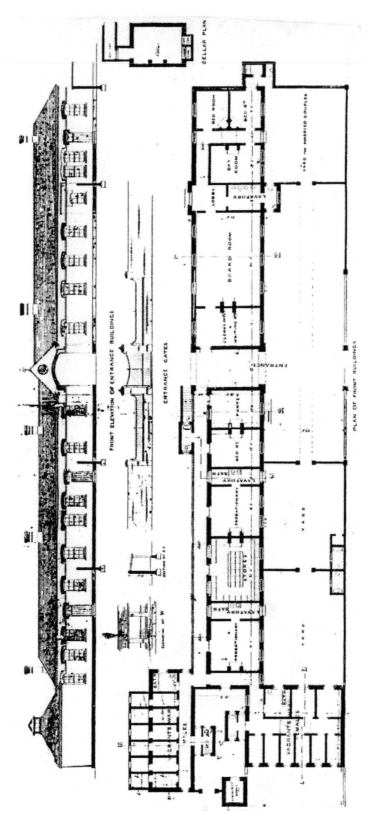

*Plan of entrance range*

*Master's House: the Morgan family and Sister Jefferson on steps. c.1920*

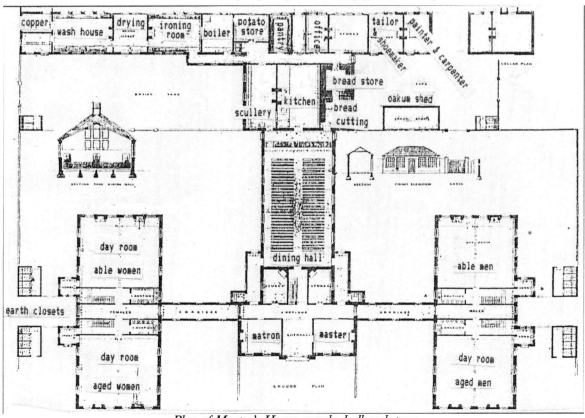

*Plan of Master's House, wards, hall and stores*

These buildings were later supplemented by the following: first the infirmary in 1882:

*The infirmary*

Note the wards for venereal disease and the male and female yards. The use of pauper nurses was not banned until 1896. The two-bed lying-in ward was for maternity cases and was superseded in 1898 by a larger building.

The children's accommodation and school was finally added in 1886. *The Christchurch Times* described the new quarters as:

*Lying-in ward*

*Well-built, of a light and airy character . . . well-appointed . . . every convenience close at hand ... Not elaborately furnished, but furniture chiefly new. In the centre of the ground floor is a schoolroom, with the governess's apartments and kitchen adjoining. On either side of the building is a day room, a work room, a bathroom and a lavatory (fitted in the running-jet system that ten might wash*

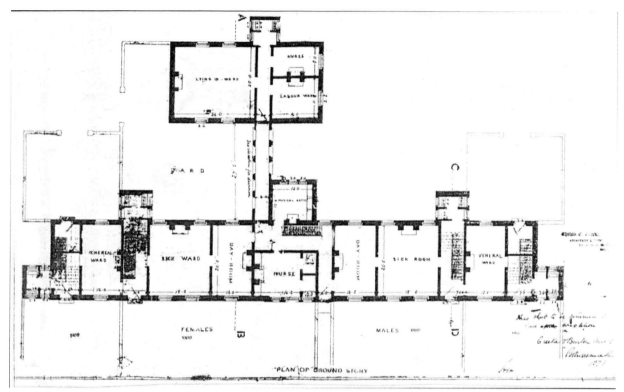

*Plan of infirmary*

at the same time). Upstairs, the rooms comprise a sick room, clothing stores and bedrooms. The girls and boys have separate but similar rooms, the boys occupying the suite of rooms on the eastern side, and the girls on the western side. There is a staircase on both sides. The present number of children in the House is 23 boys and 13 girls, but accommodation is provided for 60. The boys and girls each have a large playground which is divided by a wall, but they both enjoy an uninterrupted outlook toward the town. The children are isolated from the adults, only meeting in the dining hall at meals, their access to the House only being approached by a footpath to a door into a corridor near the able-bodied women's ward.

*The school and schoolteacher's accommodation*

This description illustrates clearly the classification system in operation in the careful division of the sexes and the efforts made to ensure that they did not come into contact with the adults; and it is also of interest now that the Jumpers area of the town is so heavily developed to envisage the area in the immediate aftermath of the Portfield Enclosure, so empty of property.

The children's accommodation was only in use for about ten years, after which it was converted to a women's infirmary. Later still it was once again used by children when it became a children's hospital ward in the NHS era. Its last use was as a day hospital for the elderly.

In 1898 a new lying-in ward replaced the smaller one behind the infirmary. There were ten beds – representing a five-fold increase in provision in the space of sixteen years. The long corridor shown in the photo was added after the women's infirmary was moved to the empty children's ward, around the same time, to link both aspects of the maternity process.

*Lying-in ward*

Other buildings on the site by the turn of the century included a huge laundry, much added to over the years, which use pauper labour; and the nurses' home at the corner of Fairmile and Jumpers Road. More of this later.

One of the first telephone systems was installed in 1886 between the Master's rooms and the school, and extended by 1889 to link up the lying-in ward and the infirmary.

# Chapter Eight

## The new regime

The following poem appeared in *The Christchurch Times* in 1895, attributed to 'Mellor':

*The workhouse opens wide its door*
*And says to all 'Come in!*
*I welcome both the sick and poor*
*And those worn out with sin.*

*'Come in, thy gentle blear-eyed sot*
*(For though no liquor's here),*
*You'll find it warm and snug, I wot,*
*Till summer doth appear.*

*'Come in, ye girls that fallen are,*
*Ye shall have doctor's care,*
*And food and drink superior far*
*To honest woman's fare.*

*'Come in, ye aged, poor and neat,*
*And live with those who swear,*
*You'll have the self-same food to eat,*
*And self-same clothes to wear.*

*'And when the ladies give their treat,*
*No difference shall be made*
*Between the vilest of the street*
*And the most virtuous maid.*

*'Ye working man, mark well my word*
*Ye neither drink nor play,*
*But, if ye keep the workhouse "bird",*
*The piper you must pay.'*

In the first year of the new House, 1881, the 'vilest' and the 'virtuous' were entered alike into the Admissions book for that year and make interesting reading. They include hawkers, laundresses, shoemakers, painters, sawyers, plasterers and labourers, alongside a 'nurse' (not entirely a respectable occupation at that time), and a sexton. A bricklayer, washerwoman, widow, housemaid, cook, butler, charwoman, servant, dressmaker and a carpenter were also in the book. But one would not expect to find a musician, a photographer or a schoolmistress, although they were there. Perhaps it really was the demon drink that brought them to the workhouse door, as was so often claimed, though not entirely without justice, by certain Guardians in those avidly pro-temperance times.

A fine example of that class of person so despised by the workhouse authorities, the so-called 'in-and-out' type, appears by the name of Charles Harvey Atkins. Mr Atkins was admitted no less than 29 times between November 1885 and October 1887, sometimes reappearing on the same day as his discharge. The name crops up again in 1896, when a man referred to as 'Atkins' was forceably ejected from the boardroom, having 'on many occasions wearied the Guardians with his petty grievances'. His particular offence on that last occasion was to have demanded of them whether they were 'Guardians of the poor or guardians of the Poor Law'. One cannot help but think it was the same man.

Other cases were plainly in the category of the virtuous: the deserted widow, the four children deserted by both parents; the two-year-old boy whose parents were in Winchester gaol and who was brought in by the police.

The fear of the workhouse by this time was very deep-seated. An inquest on an elderly man who had died just a few minutes after being admitted to the infirmary, though he had slept in a woodshed on Jumpers Common on a layer of straw, and suffered from heart disease and dropsy, was told that he would only consent to being admitted when dying on being convinced that it was to a hospital and not a workhouse that he was being taken. The Preface provides another example, of course; the reluctance in that case probably directly contributed to the child's death.

Life was indeed harsh inside. Not even old men were exempt from the requirement to work. Some of even 80 years of age had to chop wood; in 1898 the Guardians thoughtfully erected a wood-chopping shed for them in their yard. The able-bodied females were engaged as before in the laundry and housework, although it would be a mistake to consider this to have been light work. It was far more likely to have involved hours on end on hands and knees scrubbing floors. The inmate who refused to work in 1891 on account of suffering 'aches and pains' all over from scrubbing, was probably quite genuine. Nevertheless, her inability to carry out the work cost her seven days' hard labour in prison. Even infirmary inmates had to work on oakum-picking.

The able-bodied males, still the class the deterrence principle was chiefly devised for, were put on stone-breaking. They had to break up seven hundredweight of Mendip stone between the hours of 7am and 3pm. Another task was oakum-picking. When the painful fingertips this caused was brought to the attention of the Guardians they refused to believe it was true. 'To some people any work produced a disagreeable sensation,' remarked one. This task was also assigned to vagrants and led to protests from a more humane Guardian, Mr Harvey, who described it as 'distasteful and offensive'. It was meant to be, of course. Each man had to pick four pounds a day. It was not humane,' said Mr Harvey: 'They are human beings!' Such an outburst of compassion usually left the majority of Guardians unmoved, as it did on this occasion. One merely sarcastically suggested that perhaps the men should have a game of marbles or billiards instead – this from the self-same Revd Pretyman whose heart had gone out to the children at Tuckton.

Those inmates who made themselves useful were, however, given due recognition, albeit in a small way. One very helpful inmate had saved the Board a good deal of money by doing odd jobs, and after much agonising about the correct response he was rewarded with an extra ounce of tobacco each week. Conversely, the pages of the local paper are full of court cases of workhouse miscreants. Violence frequently broke out, and often involved the young women: one Annie Harris, aged 20, was lucky to get off with a caution for assaulting a fellow inmate. She threw water over her adversary and threatened to throttle her! In the young men's wards a notice had to be displayed forbidding 'blasphemous or obscene talk'. Some things never change …

There were other more desirable occupations, including work in the grounds. The strawberries grown were served up to the Guardians, but eventually they magnanimously forewent this little perk in favour of the inmates, at a later time when attitudes had softened.

The diet seemed to be reasonable. In fact, the Christchurch Union was generous in comparison with other workhouses in Hampshire, supplying precisely 27.5oz of meat each week as opposed to 17.7oz elsewhere, Such exactitude reflects the almost legalistic approach to the dietary rations then adopted. The water, which was drawn from wells, left much to be desired, being found by Dr Hartford, the Medical Officer, to be 'very bad indeed' in 1891, containing swarms of organisms. Lunatics were still kept at the House, and no proper provision ever seems to have been found for them. Reference to padded restraints and again to the Western Counties Idiot Asylum at Starcross, Exeter, are made, so, as before, some were sent away and some remained. Alcoholics were included in this category. Other ill inmates had the benefit of the infirmary, in which the medicinal use of alcohol was very common, and led to queries from the Guardians about the quantities consumed. In 1898 they had noticed that the quarterly consumption of brandy had risen in only 15 months from one gallon to 15 gallons! Although the Medical Officer was expected to find the money for medicines out of his own pocket, brandy was the exception and the ratepayers footed the bill. Perhaps the MO was taking advantage of this in avoiding prescribing remedies at his own expense. Dr Hartford did point out that some unions sent their incurable patients away, but Christchurch did not, and brandy was then an important stimulant.

A clue to the workhouse uniform is provided by a reference in the local newspaper in 1898 to blue serge being adopted for male infirmary patients instead of corduroy. A surviving tender for clothing from 1915 gives a more detailed picture for that time: men wore grey suits and blue 'slop' jackets, with cord or cloth trousers, grey worsted stockings and overcoats and hats when needed; boys wore serge sailor suits or tweed suits; both girls and boys had straw hats. No actual clothes are on the order form for women, but grey calico, stays and black worsted stockings indicate something suitably dismal, and were once more made in the House.

Numbers in the House had soon risen to a level where the buildings were just as full as the previous workhouse had been – over the planned 200 capacity by 1897. When this information was revealed in the local paper's usual reports of the board meetings, a helpful reader wrote with a kind offer to take an eligible woman off the Union's hands! His request for a wife was rejected, but gave the Guardians much amusement. They even suggested sending the man a sample. Perhaps the applicant had the last laugh, as he subsequently received over 200 offers of marriage in reply.

The question of classification still obsessed the Guardians, and in 1896 they turned their collective mind to further refinements of the divisions between the classes of adult inmates. The following is the scheme that was subsequently introduced:

The classification was sub-divided into two groups:

A(1) Men over 60 with ten years' residence in Christchurch (Union) without having claimed poor relief previously, and unable through no fault of their own to maintain themselves;

A(2) Men over 16 temporarily 'infirm' and of previous good character with residential qualifications as above; also

A(3) Widows with children, deserted wives with children, with character and residence qualifications as above.

This 'A' group was permitted privileges such as permission to walk in the grounds, frequent leave of absence, a separate table in the dining hall and better clothing (woollen suits) with no distinction or uniformity of character. Their sleeping arrangements were upgraded and divided into personal cubicles, over 7' by nearly 3' in size. Small though this space appears, it was apparently able to contain an iron washstand, folding bed, a chair, a box, a small shelf and a mirror, and was even carpeted. It was their task to keep their own cubicle tidy. The men were entitled to a tobacco allowance and the women to snuff. The Class As were given a day room, also carpeted, with the luxury of armchairs, tables, shelves – and, the crowning glory of 'coloured tablecloths'! They were also entitled to a better diet, including 2oz of tobacco each week and tea in the afternoon. From this group were selected the workhouse inmate posts of messengers, gatemen and wardsmen.

Other classes were sub-divided into a 'B' group. These were inmates over 16 of good character and who had a satisfactory reason for not being able to provide for themselves. The only alteration to the existing conditions for this group was that they had to wear old workhouse clothes, not new issue.

All other adult inmates were classed as 'C'. This group was to receive the full deterrence treatment. No privileges whatsoever; distinctive treatment in all respects; strict discipline; their existing diet was downgraded, and they had to wear a distinctive uniform 'of the oldest and worst description'. They were to be confined to their yards and had only limited leave of absence. All the most disagreeable work was to be assigned to this class and no beer or tobacco rations were given.

In a survey in that year, of the 89 inmates to be reclassified, 13 were in the top A(1) category, just one in the A(2), none in the A(3); 42 were in the B section, and 33 in the C. So it can be seen that most of the current inmates would have lost privileges and suffered worse conditions under the new scheme – which was in some respects an attempt to address the unfairness in the treatment of the 'deserving' and 'undeserving' poor which the opening poem of this chapter lampooned the year before. The well-meant attempt was not unsurprisingly met with little enthusiasm on the part of the inmates. One courageous objector even went as far as to write to the Guardians describing the Class A cubicles as 'hoss-boxes' – and this from one who was meant to feel greatly favoured!

## The workhouse children

The children had school to keep them occupied, although rather joylessly it would seem, from the observation in 1887 by Guardian Revd Clutterbuck that they though had a 'fairly creditable' examination performance, they 'appeared somewhat deficient in animation'. It is another disturbing clue to their lack of happiness that some would frequently manage to run away. One ten-year-old achieved four or five such escapes and once got as far as Ringwood. The Guardians reprimanded him, but washed their hands of the punishment, which was left entirely to the Master and can only be imagined. It was probably the birch: two unruly boys received this correction for misbehaviour in the school. They were, it appeared, beyond the control of the schoolmistress, and the episode led directly to the decision in 1892 to send the children out to school, commencing with these and other difficult boys (to the no doubt unalloyed delight of the National School ). Eight boys even managed to abscond from that school. This little group's complaints were reported in the paper: they complained of ill-treatment at the hands of the workhouse industrial trainer. All this does not suggest that the children enjoyed any emotional security. Persistently difficult children could be sent to an Industrial School (like a Borstal).

The Local Government Board inspector, Mr Baldwyn Fleming still, was very critical of the standard of care the children were receiving. He pointed out to the Guardians in 1891 that the children were dirty (despite the 'running-jet' system!), many had chilblains and skin diseases were common. The lavatories they had to use were unclean, and their beds untidily made. It does not do the officials of the time much credit.

They were expected to take their fair share of work in addition to their schooling, which typically meant domestic chores for the girls and gardening for the boys. Some effort was made to alleviate their boredom, which the Guardians did by this time at last perceive as a legitimate problem, and from about 1897 balls and bats and skipping ropes were provided, especially through Guardian Mr Cooper-Dean; also books (though a Guardian objected to this as books were only thrown around, he claimed), and toys were obtained by appeal through newspapers. Some kind and thoughtful citizens gave other items to fill their dull days with a little childish pleasure – a rocking horse or a picture book might come their way. It is sad to contemplate the lives of their predecessors without such frivolities.

Details of their diet survive and show that they had lunch at 10am, which was bread and dripping. Dinner was either bread and soup, bread and stew, pork and vegetables or beef and vegetables. On Saturdays they were given boiled rice and jam. Like modern children, they did not care for the meat. Unlike modern children, this may have been because the pork came from the workhouse's own pigs, kept on the farm opposite Fairmile, and slaughtered just beyond the kitchens.

The girls were still being trained for a life in service, and in fact demand for them exceeded supply. Many boys went to Grimsby to work in the fishing trade, an 'apprenticeship' for which the Guardians paid the smack owners a premium of £5 even though this practice was officially forbidden by the 1834 Act, and was an extremely dubious destination for their charges. They were aware that stories were in circulation about the treatment received by the boys, and that those boys who wrote to the Guardians about their conditions would only be saying what the fishing-smack owners wished them to say. When Mr Cooper-Dean questioned fellow Board members about their suspicions, they owned up to having followed up properly only one of the many apprentices sent to Grimsby. The boys were indeed asked and consented to going into the trade, but

Mr Cooper-Dean was probably quite correct when he pointed out that this was done because of romantic notions about a life at sea gleaned from Bible stories. One Christchurch lad did become the captain of a steamer; another was returned as unsuitable, his romantic notions having been rudely dispelled. When actually asked what they wished to do, out of eight boys, one wished to be a telegrapher, one a soldier, one a gardener, four sailors, and one ambitious little chap, 'nothing'. A life in the navy was indeed an alternative, many boys being sent to training ships at Southampton, and army life was also an option: more than one drummer boy originated from Christchurch Workhouse.

Provision for the youngest children was haphazard at first, until a nursery for them was established in 1895 to replace the existing arrangement of using 'the most respectable women in the wards' to mind them. Despite concern that such lavish care would encourage illegitimacy, a ward was sub-divided and a day attendant employed; at night the babies could return to their mothers if they had one. A couple of years later, six prams were obtained after a public appeal, and the days when the babies and toddlers were confined in one room all day came to an end.

The lives of the older children also improved further as the century drew to a close. The Guardians by then recognised that it was 'wrong for them to be shut away from the outside world through no fault of their own', and the great step forward of allowing them to go to school with ordinary children came in 1892. They were readily identifiable, all the same, until the distinctive workhouse garb (described by Guardian Henry West Jenkins as 'hideous') was dropped in 1895, before which the boys had to wear knickerbockers. Despite this, they still looked alike, as later pictures of them show. In the same year they began to attend Sunday School and church. Girls were given nightdresses to wear, and toothbrushes; all those seemingly minor improvements illustrate just how deprived of normal comforts and amenities the children had been up to then.

The children were still discriminated against by the authorities: in 1899 the National School demanded a fee for their attendance, something not required from ordinary town children, probably because the school was funded by voluntary contributions and sought to boost funds by billing the Guardians. No such defence can be made for the Congregational Day School in Millhams Street, whose schoolmistress, Miss Smedley, haughtily informed the Guardians that she had instructions not to admit workhouse children. It will be seen later what opposition was to come from state schools.

A great experiment was conducted in 1892 which proved to be successful: the boarding out of children. At this stage, only orphans and abandoned children could be considered for this, not the ordinary poor, so they were in a minority, but undoubtably a lucky one. At last, such children 'had something in the nature of a home', said a Guardian. Foster parents were paid a fee of £5 a week – more than most parents had to raise their children with, as the Guardians were acutely aware – and were conscientiously visited by the Ladies Visiting Committee on a regular basis. The editor of *The Christchurch Guardian* should have felt vindicated, having suggested such a solution nearly ten years earlier.

Strange to say, this arrangement was finally to account for the care of almost all workhouse children by the end of this story, but was only in its infancy then. The biggest alteration in the conditions of the children who remained in the workhouse came in 1896 with the opening of the first of the Cottage Homes.

## The Cottage Homes

The rationale behind this development was the new concern to separate the children not only from the adults but from the workhouse itself, a decision that was made by the Board in 1892. A new morality was pervading the boardroom regarding those in its care who were blameless for their plight, and even though they recognised that their plans for separate homes for groups of twenty children would cost more than putting them all in one large block, they desired to 'do what's right and best for the children'. Their decision was part of a national trend, led by Dr Barnardo. Twenty-one acres opposite the workhouse were acquired from a member of the Druitt family and four Homes and a schoolroom were swiftly constructed by W J Chinchin and ready by February 1896.

*Cottage Home*

Overall responsibility for the Homes was placed in the hands of a Superintendent and Matron: the first appointed were Henry and Alice Dyer. The Guardians had argued vehemently for control to be vested in the workhouse master, but the Local Government Board would not permit this on principle. Later developments at the Cottage Homes made this insistence, with hindsight, disastrous for the welfare of the children.

Each Home was run by an assistant matron and was set in a large plot approached by wrought iron entrance gates and pillars, the four buildings grouped around a central green as shown in the aerial photo below (c.1920). At the head of the green was the school. Two Homes were for boys and two for girls; those who had parents in the workhouse were permitted visits from them once a week, but were strictly forbidden to visit the workhouse over the road themselves. Swings and cricket balls were provided at the outset. Almost from the first day the new schoolroom was redundant as all the children went to the National School (now the Priory C of E School). The schoolmistress's services were dispensed with, but as the last school inspection revealed a 'great want of order', this was no loss. The assistant matrons taught the under-fives.

Life for the inmates generally in this period continued to be enriched from time to time courtesy of various public-spirited individuals, and on special occasions such as the 1887 Silver Jubilee and the Diamond Jubilee ten years' later. Indeed, the frequency of such events worried the Guardians, who always insisted that excursions to pantomimes etc were to be denied to the able-bodied. George Marshall (proprietor of *The Christchurch Times*) annually collected funds for the entertainment of inmates and maintained a list of subscribers which included Lord Malmesbury and some of the Guardians themselves. One year he was so incensed by the refusal of the Guardians to allow him to entertain the majority of the inmates that he cancelled the planned concert. Always the Guardian most keen to make workhouse life unvaryingly tedious, it was James Druitt's insistence that the workhouse was not 'an assembly room for concert parties', that caused the difficulty.

One kind offer received an even more contemptuous rebuff and is worth recounting at length for its hilarity value.

It began just after the move the to Fairmile, in mid-December 1881, and when the Guardians were at their most autocratic. One John Butler, of West End Farm (Castle's the ironmongers today), wrote to the

*Cottage Homes, c.1925*

Board offering to perform some of Handel's Oratorio for the inmates on Christmas Day. The Board members scoffed: the inmates 'were not quite up to Handel's music, and probably not up to whom Handel was', sneered one of them.

Their rejection duly appeared in the next Board meeting report in the local paper, prompting an enraged Mr Butler to demand an apology. Instead of getting one, all he got was hearty laughter from the Guardians, although they did have the belated courtesy to reply in writing to his offer, with thanks.

The spurned would-be benefactor was having none of it and wrote two more letters to the Board, which the clerk 'would not trouble to read' and wrote to refuse to accept any further communication.

At this point, now March 1882, the writer seemed to become unhinged. 'The pen is mightier than the sword,' he dramatically wrote the Board, and mysteriously rambled on about an eye for an eye, each man has his price, and other well-worn phrases. He concluded his diatribe by demanding £5 or an apology.

Later in March he somewhat recovered his composure, and apologised about seeking an apology, but insisted on the money being handed over. The letter was left to lie on the table, but not before it had been greeted by further contemptuous guffaws.

By April, the Guardians had ceased to see the funny side. The next letter, not revealed in the paper, had merely become 'tiresome'.

A long silence followed, after which their antagonist sent them best wishes for a happy new year. It was now 1883. More laughter.

April saw another communication from Mr Butler, this time of the unhinged variety. 'Gentlemen, I am a fool,' he announced to them. The chairman remarked that the contents of the letter 'raised no controversy' and the Board 'unanimously agreed with the sentiments of the writer'.

The final letter from poor Mr Butler was allowed to remain on the table, its contents disappointingly undisclosed to *The Christchurch Times*. It was October 1883 – nearly two years of farce.

The vagrants increased dramatically once their insalubrious new cells were opened at Fairmile, an 'ever-swelling and unsightly army of ne'er-do-wells' (*The Christchurch Times* editorial). They remained obstinately

**Mr. J. E. Holloway.**

*From a Photograph by Messrs. Debenham and Gould.*

Mr. Holloway, who is Mayor of Christchurch, has twice previously filled the office. He is also at the present time Chairman of the Christchurch Board of Guardians.

Mr. T. Beeche*

Mr. R. Sworn.

Mr. J. H. Moore.

Mr. H. W. Jenkins.

*Guardians, 1890 (Bournemouth Visitors' Directory)*

undeterred by the harshest of conditions, although they did get the benefit of heating after six chilly years, as it had been noticed that a hoar frost would form overnight on their blankets. Even when with an improvement in employment their numbers did decline, it was only remarked upon with withering scorn by the Guardians: Major Maunsell sneered that he supposed their treatment was not so good as formerly, and another raised a laugh by remarking that somehow no tramps came on Christmas Day. Later, the same sarcasm would be applied whenever similar situations arose – that Christchurch stone was too hard for them, for instance. There was never at any time any sympathy for their plight.

The workhouse had opened in 1881 with the Master and Matron, Mr and Mrs Saunderson, from the old workhouse. Before many months were out they had resigned, to be replaced by Mr Thomas and Mrs Martha Badcock, from the Woolwich Union. These two continued in their posts for only a few years, when they were replaced by Mr and Mrs Fey.

Guardians came and went: James Kemp Welch died in 1887, and John Edward Holloway became chairman. On the Board in 1890 were Messrs Holloway, Maunsell, Lane, Harvey, Proudley, Sworn, Hoare, Jenkins, Moore, Beechey, Lander, Preston, Cooper-Dean, John Kemp Welch and Aldridge. Many of these people served year after year without their election being contested. So time-wasting did annual elections become that they were replaced in that year by triennial ones. *Ex-officio* members for that year were Lord Malmesbury, Captain Elwes and Mr Eyre. These posts were abolished in 1894.

A major personnel problem that dogged the Christchurch Guardians and to which they never found the solution nor the cause of was the difficulty in obtaining and keeping nurses. Accommodation was a problem that was initially addressed by providing them with beds in the former children's quarters. Though a nurses' home was built at the corner of Fairmile and Jumpers Road in 1902, when there were only eight nurses, neither this facility nor any other made any difference. Various explanations were put forward: that Christchurch was too dull for them (so they were provided with a piano which on later enquiry the Guardians found none of them could play); it was far too far for them to walk from the nurses' home to the infirmary (so they were provided with Ulster coats and spare uniforms); salary was too low – it was increased; work was too exhausting – ward maids provided. To no avail. A squabble with an inmate about the exact position of her leafless pot plant led to the huffy resignation of one Nurse Manser, who the wrote to *The Christchurch Times* complaining of the staff indiscipline and bickering, and went off to seek another occupation, 'tired of the Poor Law'. By 1904 a nurse was resigning at almost each Board meeting. It cannot have helped that the Board was so strict about them: all the outside doors of the workhouse were locked after 9pm, and even though the nurses complained about the effect this had on their social lives, it was a regulation that was not lifted. Something had to be done: in 1913 it was decided that the workhouse should train its own nurses, but, as we shall see, the problem continued into the era of the welfare state.

Bournemouth and Christchurch both grew rapidly; new electoral wards and districts were constantly springing up. Some of them, e.g. Winton and Springbourne, housed the working people who were the main users of the workhouse. The committees spawned by the Board grew relentlessly: there was a Finance Committee, School Attendance Committee, Vaccination Committee, Assessment Committee (rates), Relief Committee, Workhouse Committee, Classification Committee, Ladies Visiting Committee, and a Buildings Committee (not an exhaustive list), all of which in the words of a 'Long-Suffering Ratepayer' writing to *The Christchurch Times*, 'vie with each other in adding expense to expense'. Even one of the Guardians, Mr Preston was worried. Christchurch, he said, was 'constantly being told that it was the most expensive, most extravagant, yet best-kept workhouse in the country.'

This last smug comment was severely tested by a major scandal that hit the Guardians in 1890 – which, once again, arose from the negligence of a Medical Officer.

# Chapter Nine

## The public enquiry

In September 1890, a Nurse Sarah Matkin wrote a courageous letter of complaint to one of the Guardians, Major Maunsell, and thereby set in train events that shook the Board out of its cosy complacency.

'Two lawyers and a couple of parsons, a number of builders and estate agents, a few farmers and a sprinkling of tradesmen, an officer and a couple of country squires, with one or two of the nondescript class called gentlemen, and you have our Board.' This withering assessment was made by a Guardian, the Revd Cleale, under a pseudonym, in *The Christian Magazine*. Although it relates to 1896, the composition of the Board had hardly altered since the Great Scandal six years earlier.

The nurse's complaint about the treatment of a patient, brought to her in the infirmary 'more in the manner of a dog than a human being', was of sufficient weight to postpone the funeral and order a coroner's inquest. The coroner ordered an investigation, news of which was printed in *The Christchurch Times* and *The Bournemouth Directory* and afterwards in *The Salisbury and Winchester Journal*. The scandal even reached the ears of the London reporters, who in *The London Star* referred to the 'simply shameful' situation of a 'poor old man dying in a workhouse without attention or food'. Newspapers loved workhouse scandals, of which there was a plentiful supply, and the more lurid the better for sales.

*The probationary ward where John Campbell was examined*

The gist of the accusations was that an inmate was admitted through illness but died after three days without having received medical attention or food. There are both heroes and villains in this story, but it is basically one of mistakes and mismanagement, rather than deliberate cruelty.

At the insistence of the Local Government Board, Mr Baldwyn Fleming came down from London to conduct the enquiry, which was very professionally handled and lasted three days. Many witnesses were called, both inmates and staff.

The inquiry heard that one John Campbell, a wheelwright-cum-carpenter, of Christchurch, aged 60, had come to the workhouse on account of ill-health, and therefore, inability to work, on a Friday in September. He had seen the porter, Eli Troke, and had the obligatory bath, after which he was examined by the then Medical Officer, Dr Legate. Readers may remember the same gentleman attending the case of the dying child which was the subject of the Preface. The doctor gave Mr Campbell a brief check-up, and directed him to the old men's ward. In fact, the man was suffering from heart disease, as the doctor must have known as he had checked his pulse, and should have been sent straight to the infirmary.

It was observed by a witness that Campbell could barely put one foot in front of the other when he came into the ward.

Once left in the ward, Campbell's condition caused his fellow inmates serious concern: he was far too ill to get up to go to the dining hall for food, and the other inmates had too much fear of the officers and wardsmen to ask for help for him. Even a glass of water, which he had begged for, was refused by the porter, who told another inmate that only the Master could authorise such a request to be granted. Campbell was by the Sunday pleading for food, moaning, gasping, with cold hands and feet, blue lips, and in great pain. He asked why it was that 'they should be so cruel to me; I never had a shilling out of them all of my life.'

Campbell did get to the infirmary in the end – slung over the porter's back and carried in this manner down the stairs and through the long corridors. On reaching the infirmary at last, he died within ten minutes. Dr Legate issued a death certificate without having seen the body, giving the cause of death as angina.

The negligence of the doctor is obvious. Had he given Campbell the attention his illness demanded he might have lived longer, or at least died with due care and attention.

Other workhouse officials plainly showed themselves in a most unfavourable light: the porter who was surly and rude and who Nurse Matkin accused of 'gross and wilful neglect' (not an overstatement, in view of the refusal of a glass of water to a dying man); the Master, Mr Fey, who should have toured the wards each night but did not; the schoolmistress and the industrial trainer who plainly lied about having seen Campbell in the dining hall eating his dinner; the Guardians who were not sure if they were within their rights to actually set foot in and inspect the workhouse which they governed every aspect of (in fact, only those Guardians actually serving on the Visiting Committee had this right), and in particular, James Druitt, who tried to make out that Campbell had merely caught a cold on his final journey through the damp meadows – always the most eager apologist for the system.

The inspector, Mr Fleming, quite rightly ruled that those responsible for the scandal should pay the price. The Master, Mr Fey, he dismissed, along with the Matron and the porter. They had all been informed that Campbell was unable to leave his bed, but none of them had taken responsibility for attending to him.

Mr Fleming also demanded the dismissal of Dr Legate, who showed 'culpable carelessness' in the initial diagnosis of his patient, and in the lack of instructions as to diet or treatment. Unbelievably, the Guardians strongly resisted this order, but were obliged to carry it out. Their protests did, however, result in Dr Legate being allowed to keep his post as the District Medical Officer, dealing with the recipients of out-relief. Although Dr Legate is often remembered in the town as the 'Friend to the Poor', his professional conduct in this and the case in the Preface does him no credit, and a daughter of one of the Guardians, writing to the author in 1997, remembered him as being 'rather bad' – as a medical man.

Improvements were made as a result of this public examination of the failings of the workhouse management. The subsequent Masters and Matrons were now obliged to attend at each meal in the dining hall and visit each inmate twice daily. The Visiting Committee inspected the House weekly, and made surprise visits to the wards to question the inmates directly without the Master or Matron being present. The infirmary nurse was given a nursing assistant and was permitted to carry a supply of brandy as a stimulant instead of having to order it through the Medical Officer. The inmates got a clock in the wards and specific instructions about the use of the bell to summon help, which they had all been afraid to use before.

From a staggering total of 74 applicants, a new Master and Matron, Mr Harry and Mrs Laura Found, were appointed. A new porter and 'cook' (really, the porter's assistant, helping to wash the female vagrants) were also appointed at the same time. Not much later Mrs Found and the porter were each complaining about the other's rudeness, so it seemed that one rude porter was exchanged for another.

Mr Fey, whom the Guardians regarded as having been far too severely punished by the inspector, was selected as Vaccination Officer for the Union, the Guardians feeling genuine concern that he would face ruin as a result of his dismissal.

As for the heroine, Nurse Matkin, who alerted the authorities to the appalling case of Mr Campbell, she lasted two more years at the institution before being invited to resign for the crime of playing cards with the inmates. She had brought to the attention of the Guardians not only this case, which she said was 'not the first', but other shortcomings such as underweight rations. But, such is the sweetness of revenge, and so often it seems that those who act courageously and altruistically in exposing the abuses they witness are only appreciated for their actions long after the event, by posterity – when posterity is made aware of it. But for her, many other inmates would have suffered neglect and ill-treatment, and the officials would have blithely carried on failing to fulfil their duties to their charges.

The inquiry proved of great interest in adding to our knowledge about workhouse routine. The inmates would file into the hall (under the inscription intended to inspire rapt gratitude: 'God Bless our Workhouse Master') for their meals. Breakfast was at 6.30am in summer, 7.30am in winter. Dinner, in the middle of the day, consisted of pork, potatoes and turnips. The bell for them to leave off work rang at 5pm; supper was at six. Grace was said before supper, everyone having to stand, before sitting down to a repast of precisely 6oz of bread, $1^3/_4$ oz of cheese, and a pint of tea. Each table was allowed only two mugs for however many people were sitting at it, so they had to share (until as a result of the inquiry they got a mug each). The bell rang again for bed at 8pm; the men had to put out the gas lamps themselves before retiring.

Inmates grumbled to each other about the stone-breaking, were loyal to one another – one who would not leave Campbell to attend the Sunday service was summoned for 'cheek' to Mrs Fey's office – and a crippled man had to be placed in with the aged men in their ward because of the taunts he received from the young men.

From about this time, conditions in the House slowly improved. The bored old men were employed in an early form of occupational therapy known as the 'Brabazon scheme', by which they made baskets, rugs, wickerwork, woollen clothing and suchlike under the tutelage of the Ladies Visiting Committee, ably led and initiated by Mrs Risdon Sharp, wife of the prominent local solicitor of Millhams Meade. The committee began in 1895 and consisted of thirteen ladies who visited all the women and children. Their reports were initially treated by the Guardians with their characteristic and virtually automatic contempt; for instance, when the ladies pointed out that the meat was too hard for the inmates too eat, the Guardians were greatly astonished and accused them of being too tender-hearted. Mrs Sharp was a force to be reckoned with, however. She was one of the first women Guardians and had a genuine interest in the poor, travelling miles from house to house on foot to visit the sick and infirm.

The men in the Brabazon scheme received payment in kind, e.g. extra tobacco, and each year the results of their labours were sold in the boardroom to raise funds for new materials or to provide extras for the wards, for example, a gramophone. The women were not as fortunate: they 'had their full employ in other work'. This would most likely refer to the laundry or dressmaking.

The old men got another perk in 1895: a smoking room. Elsewhere, smoking was banned, especially for the loathed able-bodied men. Some people showed that they could never be happy, no matter what – two men ended up in prison when they fought with one another because non-smokers were in the smokers' room. Today, it would be the other way round.

The old women got benches in their yards, and a supply of tea, milk and sugar to have the freedom of making a hot drink when they wanted one. Guards were put on the heaters in the wards for the poor laundry women who were attempting to dry their wet feet on them, and who had no other footwear but the boots. Not that this modest variation in the policy of deterrence did not meet with howls of protest from some quarters. A correspondent, 'Christchurch Ratepayer', to *The Christchurch Times,* bewailed this new liberality:

> *It is pretty nigh time that the Guardians began to consider whether the luxuries and treats to the inmates of the workhouse had not gone nearly far enough ... in addition to having well nigh a palace to live in, the Guardians are anxious to make the mode of life in the workhouse palatial also. The treatment of the inmates, children and all, is much more than coddling. It is feasting galore and housing luxurious! Why,* even Mr Druitt [my emphasis] *is suggesting slippers – not yet dressing-gowns for the poor overworked laundrywomen in the House.*

Times were moving on, however.

The appearance of the workhouse continued to change for the better. Mr Cooper-Dean generously donated one hundred trees for the grounds in 1897, and the Guardians completed their last building for the century – the lying-in ward (F Ward in the last days of the hospital use), with beds for ten mothers. All was set for the workhouse to go into the 20th century, but not without one last gasp from the diehards. When Dr Hartford asked for fixed baths for the infirmary instead of the existing wheeled one, Mr Druitt was appalled: 'Fixed baths are a source of considerable danger,' he fulminated.

The new spirit abroad was ably expressed by a Guardian, the Revd Cleale, writing, as previously mentioned, under a pseudonym in 1896:

> *We call our board a progressive one ... we keep pace with the times and we have the humanising tendencies of the day well represented. We treat our aged and sick as kindly as a Poor Law that badly needs reform will allow us. Our children go to the National School and can hardly be said to be clothed in uniform. Cottage Homes are in the course of erection. Non-Conformists and Roman Catholics hold a religious service in the House. A Ladies Visiting Committee sees to a good deal that the Guardians would never observe. Our relief is fairly, judiciously given, and when the Local Government Board sent down a circular recommending the classification of, paupers according to character and conduct ... we set to work at once.*

> *Of course, we differ very much ...* [There are] *great distinctions between the old-school Guardians who are still wedded to the principles of the Poor Law Act of 1834, and the new humanitarian school. Not but what the old school members are humane enough in their own way - one of the most rigid is often ready enough with a little bit of help out of his own pocket to a case the Board cannot touch, but they act on a different principle.*

> *They are terribly afraid of making pauperism too attractive ... Do away with uniforms? Why? They are paupers and you can't make them any other. Remove the children from the workhouse surroundings? Stuff and nonsense! The children have always turned out well ...*

> *The old-school Guardians have a great dislike to paupers adding to their miserable pay by taking any kind of remunerative employment ...* [it] *seems very hard that a widow with four or five children and not 10s a week to keep them, may not put a few things in her window, or let part of her house, or take in a little washing ...*

> *It is hard to be a conscientious Guardian, to steer straight between inclination and duty, between the humanity that would deal tenderly and the mistaken kindness that encourages pauperism and sets a premium on vice. It is difficult to help the unfortunate without encouraging the idle.*

The aged had won some understanding and consideration; sympathy for the young pauper was far less forthcoming: '... modern Poor Law administration made the House, for old folks, a kind of almshouse in which they might end their days in peace and comfort. The whole system of the Poor Law has changed since its beginning and changed for the better in regard to the aged and infirm. They [the Guardians] could make up for the increased comforts of the old people by being extra hard on the young,' Guardian Mr Whigham told a Board meeting to enthusiastic 'hear hear's.

With this ominous message to the young-able-bodied, so many of whom were soon to perish in the bloodbaths of the Somme etc, the Guardians entered the new century.

# Chapter Ten

# The Edwardian era

The first building project of the new century were the nurses' home. At the time they were having to sleep in the infirmary. Guardian A J Abbott, in the discussions preceding its construction, remarked that 'they were all exceedingly desirous to obtain for the sick and suffering poor people the best possible attention, and unless they had good nurses they could not get that attention, and if they did not provide proper accommodation they could not get nurses.' It occupies (to date, probably not for much longer) the corner of Jumpers Road and Fairmile, and was completed in 1902. Guardian Toop was outraged, calling it a 'mansion'. From a start of eight nurses there were 27 by 1926. The training school was started in 1913 because the recruitment of skilled nurses was so difficult; its unpromising beginnings would not have indicated how successful it was to become in much later years.

A new boardroom was also added in 1902 for the accommodation of the ever-increasing number of Guardians. Its construction necessitated the demolition of the married quarters, but this was not entirely regretted by the Guardians as they were aware that some of the craftier old people were marrying in the workhouse solely to improve on their accommodation! The boardroom put a stop to that sort of nonsense. The Guardians could now enter the site through their own entrance from Jumpers Road (recently defaced with official planning consent). Guardian Mr Toop characteristically called the new boardroom 'scandalous … a wanton waste of money', but others were pleased as the old one got unpleasantly full of tobacco smoke and the new one had a proper internal ventilation system.

*Nurses' Home*

*The Guardians' entrance (original door replaced by window)*

The Board also discussed a new laundry to replace that in the row of workrooms between the dining hall and the infirmary (eventually constructed in 1912) and further vagrants' wards, which were eventually built, but their time was taken up for more than ten years by the question of a new infirmary, arguments for and against which dragged on all this time with delay after delay and frequent changes of mind.

The steady increase in the numbers of inmates was the principal reason for going ahead. Numbers kept on reaching new highs: 288 in 1908; nearly 300 in 1913. The main cause of the postponement and indecision was the national legislation regarding the introduction of old age pensions, the effect of which would, it was felt, remove the need for further infirmary provision, and in the ultimate scenario lead to the abolition of the workhouse altogether – something taken seriously enough to be the recommendation of the minority report in 1909 of a Royal Commission on the Poor Law and Unemployed. In fact, these concerns took many years to be realised, as the pensions were initially restricted to those who had not received poor relief during the previous *twenty years*.

The site for the new infirmary was bought in 1905 from Lord Malmesbury, who sold to the Guardians six acres adjacent to the existing buildings, a site graphically described by Mr Cooper-Dean as 'one of the most disagreeable and unsuitable in Hampshire. On one side the cemetery, on the other the mortuary, and in front, the sewerage farm'.

Political debate about the future of the Poor Law led to resolutions to defer the infirmary and then these resolutions would be rescinded at the next Board meeting. Small wonder that Mr Druitt lost all patience: 'It was a fact', he said, 'that at one meeting some five or six Guardians came and next another set came and reversed the business done at the former meeting, and the consequence was that there was no continuity of works.' Boardroom dissension even spilled over into the press, with chairman Mr Kemp Welch and Mr A J Abbott conducting an argument in the correspondence columns of *The Christchurch Times*.

Meanwhile, the infirmaries were bursting at the seams, and people were having to be discharged prematurely. The infirmaries were 'more and more looked upon as a poor person's hospital,' observed the Master. The Medical Officer, Dr Batley, was most concerned that the overcrowding meant that ordinary patients had to be mixed in with lunatics who shouted all night and must have been exceedingly irritating, to say the least, for the inmates, if not downright terrifying. This situation continued until the new laundry was built just before the first world war, and the 'lunatics' were housed in the old one.

At last matters came to a ahead with a visit from the very capable Local Government Board inspector, Mr Baldwyn Fleming. He was able to persuade the Guardians that they had 'a clear duty' to provide the extra infirmary accommodation so desperately needed. Failure to do so might lead to the breaking away of Bournemouth as a separate union, allowing other, poorer parishes to join in with Christchurch. Although this advice was dismissed by Mr Toop as 'moonshine', Mr Fleming's, sensible approach gave the Guardians the confidence to proceed. He had explained to them that their fears about the cost, estimated to be about £20,000, were immaterial: since the workhouse was built in 1881, when there was a population in the Union of 29,847, and the last figures available from 1901, when the population had reached 69,339, the cost of relief had decreased by $\frac{1}{2}$d per head. The infirmary would, in fact, add only $\frac{1}{4}$d to the rates. (Interestingly, it was shown in the discussions that total expenditure since the new workhouse was inaugurated was £50,395.)

Mr Fleming then retired, after many years of giving the Guardians sound advice, and chiding where necessary. His successor was Mr John Walter Thompson.

In 1910 the architect, Edgar Burton once again, was instructed, and a tender for £8,641 was accepted from Jones and Seaward of Bournemouth, and the new male infirmary, now H Block, was opened in January of 1913 by the wife of the chairman, Mrs Kemp Welch, receiving this accolade from *The Christchurch Times*.

> *... new, up-to-date, magnificent ... Built of red brick and Victoria stone, roofed with Portmadoc slates, with floors of polished maple blocks and ... wards heated with the latest pattern combustible stoves, and there is a complete installation of electric lighting. There is an excellent kitchen, lavatories etc, and the walls of the building are thoroughly distempered. The infirmary has two verandahs on the west side; one end points due south, and the rooms are devoted to tubercular disease. There are twelve wards, the largest of which on the ground floor in 98' long, and the two large ones upstairs 60' and 36' feet respectively. There are 86 beds, all fitted up in the latest and most comfortable style.*

The photograph below shows the building entirely without the high workhouse walls, which had been a feature of this institution for about 150 years, and illustrates in architectural terms the profound alteration in official attitudes towards the underprivileged, as we would call them today.

*The men's infirmary*

Tea was served to 'eminent visitors, and a 'sumptuous' tea laid on for the inmates, with apples, oranges and sweets distributed, followed by a concert in the dining hall.

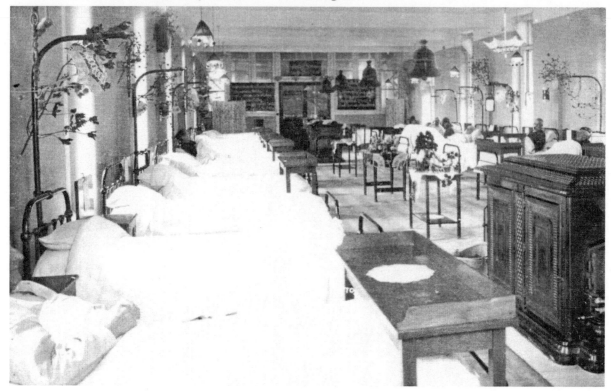

*Ward in men's infirmary*

With this lavish new provision for the men, the old infirmary (then also for men) became the quarters for aged women and married couples (who therefore lost that provision for just over a dozen years), with the little lying-in ward attached used as a work room. As the new occupants were in the favoured aged category, the walls of the yard were reduced in height to 4', from the standard 6' previously, and topped with trellis work – a sort of partial view beyond the yard thus being allowed them.

The following year, the name 'workhouse' was dropped in favour of the alternative, 'Fairmile House', as a concession to those born there who would otherwise bear a stigma on their birth certificate, but not before another reactionary Guardian had called out his own suggestion: 'How about Crockett's Hotel?' – a reference to the incumbent Master.

The shame of having to go into the workhouse ran very deep. In 1902 a hero from the Crimea war, by the memorable name of Cornelius Everett, was 'compelled' to end his days there by 'sheer want', reported *The Star*. No funds were available to assist naval men, and he had a horror of the workhouse. A man charged in 1913 with failing to maintain his children was ordered by the magistrates to remove them from the workhouse, or go in himself. 'I don't want to go back to that horrible place,' he roundly declared, preferring to abandon his children and spend a month in prison. One elderly lady committed suicide rather than go into the workhouse infirmary – an echo of the action of Tabitha Glasbery over a century earlier. The separation of couples was still practised up to the outbreak of World War One, as shown by the complaint made by an inmate whose wife had just died in the workhouse. She had been sent, he said, into the young women's ward, which he described as an 'ice-well' (there was certainly no heating in any of the ward bedrooms), pronounced fit for work (needlework), and died a month later of cirrhosis of the liver. He had not been able to visit her, nor even

*The institution c.1935 with Cottage Homes in distance*

allowed to ask. To complain, he said, meant 'Winchester [prison] staring you in the face'. It sheds doubt on the permanence of the improvements set in train after the 1890 inquiry, if inmates could still be too terrified of the consequences to ask favours from officials.

Still, conditions were steadily improving in other ways. Despite the typical resistance of Mr Druitt, another Guardian, Mr Nugent, purchased out of his own pocket a supply of newspapers. Mr Druitt was appalled: it was humbug, he said, to provide inmates with newspapers; they would be wanting other luxuries next. On some occasions, the Guardians clubbed together to assist a deserving applicant – in this way a one-legged hawker received the means to return to his native Yorkshire.

Diet got better: the bread was no longer rationed and tea was offered at breakfast as an alternative to cocoa. At one Christmas, so much food was supplied that one inmate died from excessive eating. This disclosure at the inquest so enraged a ratepayer that he wrote to ask how such a thing could happen, when in the country as a whole one hundred people died of starvation each year – some of them receiving old age pensions.

The numbers of the able-bodied paupers was worrying, particularly young women who came into the House several times to have a child but refused to give the clerk the name of the father, so that maintenance could be sought from him. Bournemouth seemed to have a bad reputation in this respect – the largest proportion of illegitimate births of all towns. Mr Cooper-Dean thought that the current enlarging of the laundry where such recalcitrant women had to work would 'put a stop to it', but it did not, and the nursery became very overcrowded. Eventually the situation was eased by sending the little ones over to the Cottage Homes once they were two, instead of at three as before.

Contemporary events are often referred to in the newspaper reports of Board meetings. An obstinate elderly woman who had been sleeping rough appeared before them in 1908. She refused to speak to the Board and was given notice to leave the workhouse. Mr Newman, a member of the Board, recommended that she joined the Suffragettes!

It was in this period that female emancipation was more directly experienced by the Guardians with the election of the first lady members in 1901. Mrs Risdon Sharp, who inaugurated the Brabazon scheme, and a Mrs Berry, were elected, to be followed by Mrs Alice Shave and Mrs Kate Grimes. It was their arrival that speeded up the humanising process far more than slow parliamentary reform. It was Mrs Grimes's resolution that out-relief was to be paid for children (in 1908) and who acidly commented that this 'had only one defect, and that was because it was proposed by a woman'; Mrs Grimes who publicised in the press the case of a 'beautiful boy' in the workhouse nursery who needed adoption; and Mrs Grimes who led the way on the Board doing whatever it could within its powers to alleviate unemployment. She also had a ready answer to the male Guardians who thought that she could not be their equal: when her membership of the Buildings Committee was queried, in that she might not know anything about foundations etc, she defended her abilities and then quietly added: 'Besides, I have served twenty years' apprenticeship to an architect as his wife'. Latter-day feminists will also relish her comment to her male colleagues regarding three men who went into police custody for not performing their tasks: 'Then the men are not *all* good!'

Mrs Shave was also a determined and caring lady. She arranged for the Cottage Homes children to get a donkey and cart for outings, and organised the appeal for this herself, despite the usual sarcasm from the other Guardians – 'How about a motor car? ... or a liveried servant?', they quipped. She understood the needs of children who would have to leave the close confines of the Homes without a friend outside and arranged for them to make return visits. Her influence was felt to be so powerful in the boardroom that when she was absent on account of her husband's illness, Board member Mr Abbott said that it did not feel like a meeting of the Guardians without her. One of her principle concerns was the plight of the unmarried mother, about which problem she read a paper to the Conference of Women Councillors, Guardians and Magistrates at Exeter in 1922; she was at the time the vice-chairman of the Board. She explained the Board's policy, which was to permit the mother if she could obtain a satisfactory placement, to leave the baby in the House and she would contribute to its maintenance. There was, she said, a Rescue Committee of twelve ladies living in the Union, of which she was Hon. Secretary: 'We have a small voluntary fund, from which we assist mothers and babies with clothing and pocket money, etc, so as to give the girls a start in beginning again and another chance.' Later in the paper, she comments that 'The thing that astonishes me, and it is *pathetic*, to find that so many girls are absolutely friendless, and it is this very friendlessness makes them too ready to accept advances from anyone to relieve the loneliness,' – a probable cause of the high rate of illegitimate Bournemouth births.

These ladies must certainly have blown much-needed fresh air through the boardroom. Mr Toop was still a Guardian at 88 years old after 30 years on the Board. He then retired but was co-opted a few weeks' later back on the Board! He died the following year, 1913. John Kemp Welch was also a Board member in excess of 28 years by that year.

The Master and Matron for many years from 1898 were a Mr and Mrs Alfred Crockett ('splendid officials', said Guardian Mr Nethercote, 'the most valuable servants the Board has ever had'); by 1905 there were 34 officials, including the clerk, five medical officers, a chaplain, a superintendent matron at the Cottage Homes, assistant matrons and nurses.

As for the casuals, their numbers were also remorselessly rising. The town mains water scheme of 1904 and the tramway works the following year brought many into the town in quest of work. A survey of 1904 showed that their numbers had increased dramatically in twenty years, from a total of 37 in 1884 to a total of 308 in that year. The majority were aged 30-40, closely followed by the 60-70 age group and the 50-60s. Most were men; there were a few children. These were sometimes dragged along by a vagabond parent to boost their funds through the sympathy factor.

In the casual wards, the men were having to sleep two to a cell. There was a brief labour shortage at the time, but Mr Crockett told the Guardians that the casuals were outcasts that no one would employ. Their diet remained dull and inadequate – bread and cheese if they remained all day on task work, dry bread if not. The same hard work was exacted: 14cwt of hard stone or one ton of soft stone to be broken up each day. They defiantly sang the following ditty whilst engaged on this task:

*Mrs Crockett, left; Mr Crockett, centre*

*Workhouse staff c.1900 on steps of Master's House*

*'The sailor loves the sea and the soldier loves the camp,*
*But give to me the King's Highway and I'll lives and dies a tramp!'*

They were not exactly made to feel welcome. Only the prospect of being arrested for 'sleeping out in the open without visible means of support', for which offence they could expect seven days hard labour in prison, could have obliged them to seek shelter here. They persisted with the traditional tramp protests of tearing up their clothes, and continued to receive the usual response from the authorities – a prison sentence. Occasionally, a more violent protest was recorded, such as by a man who broke down his cell door. 'Prison is much better than the workhouse wards,' he shouted, probably entirely justified, as he was led away from court to commence fourteen days' hard labour. Sometimes tramps simply ran off; this incurred the risk of appearing in front of the magistrates accused of the theft of workhouse clothes to the value of 25s.

Both the casuals and the able-bodied were also put to work on the workhouse land, which amounted to some twelve acres in 1899. A horse and cart were purchased at this time to assist in the cultivation. Typically, the purchase of an account book soon followed in which to keep a careful record of the work the horse was doing over on the fields behind the Cottage Homes. Not much seems to have been achieved except the waste of ink, as the farm was described in 1910 as being in a disgraceful state. There were no able-bodied men to work it, and those who could be found seemed to have no idea – one man told to weed the marrows chopped them off instead (or was this done in spite?).

With the advent of the new Insurance Act in 1912, at least those in possession of such insurance were excused the stone-breaking. The stone, incidentally, came from Shepton Mallett at a cost of 7s 2d a ton, and was sold after breaking to the Christchurch Rural District Council for 7s 11d a ton.

A hilarious misfortune befell a lady in 1904. She cannot have been of a very personable appearance, as although she was only a visitor, she was mistaken for a new inmate and plunged into a bath used nightly by vagrants. This 'brutal outrage', she said, 'had ruined her for life.' She was all of 76 years of age.

The children in the Cottage Homes were sometimes said to be better off than outside children, even according to the local education committee. A Guardian visiting from Dudley Union was 'astonished to find such luxurious places provided for poor children'.

They had the donkey cart, through the efforts of Mrs Shave, and were given drill instruction every Saturday in the empty schoolroom. This was later kitted out as a gym, with hanging rings, Indian clubs, dumbbells, parallel bars, and mattresses made by workhouse labour. There were outings every year paid for by the Board to such places as Chewton Glen, and other distractions, such as tea and sports with the mayor. A Scout troop was formed in 1911, and only two years later they won first prize at the Hampshire Scout Camp at Netley, to where they had marched 15 miles there and back.

The Blakeboroughs came to the Cottage Homes as Superintendent and Matron in 1901, and quickly made an impact on the Guardians who saw them as 'capable, efficient and painstaking'. A house was built for them in 1902 by Jenkins and Sons at a cost of £1,020, and a store adjoining for £582. The Homes themselves were filled to capacity and over, more than 100 children was not unusual. Because of this, it was decided to construct two more Homes, one each for boys and girls, but the outbreak of war was to delay this.

The Blakeboroughs stopped the children from running all over the road and going into the little thatched cottages that then lined Fairmile Road on the way to school in the town; now they walked neatly in procession. These times are now in living memory, and the sight of the Cottage Homes children being marched to school is well-remembered, as were the Blakeboroughs, who were, in fact, a grim and intimidating pair, very strict.

Destinations after the Homes remained the same – for boys, the army or navy, or apprenticeships, and the girls went into service. A new prospect was available for boys from 1910: emigration to Canada to live with families and work on their farmsteads.

The fishing trade was another outlet. In 1913 an ex-Cottage Homes lad who had joined a Brixham fleet five years before saved the life of a fellow apprentice. The Guardians were extremely impressed and decided to nominate him for an award from the Royal Humane Society. Although this could not proceed, the Guardians decided to make their own award to him, and presented him at the Cottage Homes with a silver watch and

*Teddy Porter with donkey cart*

*Ralph Blakeborough*

*The Superintendent's house*

chain, medal and Bible. 'A fine specimen of a young Englishman', *The Christchurch Times* called him. His name was William Tiller.

Those boys who found other apprenticeships were considered by the Guardians to have opportunities that were not available to many other children, but the chance they were given did not always prove to be to their advantage. A Boscombe bootmaker would not give the Guardians their premium back when his apprentice absconded. The poor boy was badly overworked, his hours being from 8am to 1pm, then 2pm until 5pm, and then again from 5.30pm until 9pm – nearly a twelve-hour day. He was beaten and his wages were not paid. This was in 1911; he was 18. Alan Druitt (clerk to the Guardians) argued that the boy was not overworked, but the case was found against the bootmaker – not for mistreatment but for failing to fulfil the conditions of the apprenticeship.

This sorry tale was matched by the typical life of a girl in service. In 1908, the minutes of the Visiting Committee recorded one aged 14 learning to make baskets and chairseats and to keep the house tidy. She was up at 6am, began work at 7am, so had to last two hours before breakfast at 8am. She then worked from 9am until 1pm; 2pm until 5pm, then after tea from 6pm to 6.30. Even then she was not finished, as she then read to her employer until 8pm, before going to bed at 9pm – a ten-hour day. This child described herself as 'happy and contented'.

A little girl of just four years old was a new arrival at the Cottage Homes in 1911, and in old age still had vivid memories of her first encounter with the Matron, Mrs Blakeborough. On account of her mother's illness, her father had to bring her and her little sisters to the Homes; they walked the five miles from Winton. It must have been heartbreaking for the father. On her way, the child picked the flowers from the hedgerows as a bouquet to present to her 'hostess' on arrival. Mrs Blakeborough remained unmoved by this childish attempt to please, and disposed of the offering in the nearest wastebin, before the child's astonished eyes.

She was then ordered to strip and put on the workhouse garb – this under the curious and very public gaze of fellow inmates.

Other aspects of life in the Homes were just as vividly brought to her mind, over eighty years later. Overcrowding was so bad that the children had to sleep two to a bed, nose to tail. Breakfast was porridge – only without either milk or sugar, therefore, just gruel; by the time she reached school she and her companions were already so hungry that they would fight over scraps of food discarded by the road. Tea was a thick slice of bread, with either margarine or jam – not both, together with a mug of cocoa. By the time she left the Homes, she was in her words 'a proper skeleton'.

Since the first edition of this book was published, further accounts of the conditions for the children in the Homes came to light as a result. The extracts above relates to memories up to the World War One period – later accounts appear in Chapter Twelve. The records of the Visiting Committee only survive for a few years in this pre-war period, but the observations they contain only indicate that matters were far more serious than the above account suggests. Three examples suffice as examples of the brutality of the Cottage Home junta:

*Mrs Elizabeth Banks of Winton, widow, applied for the discharge to her of her two children, John aged 11 and Elizabeth aged 9 years and she complained that her daughter has been found to be suffering from bruises on her back having been beaten by the Assistant Matron for being late for breakfast.*

*The clerk reported that … he received complaint from Mrs Crocker of Pokesdown that her son William aged 7 had received injury caused by a blow on the mouth … the Medical Officer found he had a bruise on the upper lip of recent origin and that two of the front teeth are loose. … Miss Macey the Matron of [No. 1] Home inflicted punishment on him with a hairbrush for failing to make use of the W.C.*

*Kathleen Crocker [aged 12] attended 'and stated she ran away from the Cottage Homes because Miss Stagg the Matron is so unkind and talks of her mother before her and that Miss Stagg said to her that the name of Crocker stinks, all the children being present and that it was while they were doing work after dinner washing up and that on a previous occasion some time ago Miss Stagg said she would sooner kick her out of the Homes than have her there and that was on the occasion when she ran away'.*

In the first case the mother was allowed to remove her children. In the second case the mother was advised by the Guardians that the injury was caused by accident. In this last case the action taken was to transfer Kathleen to another of the Homes, and that this was on account of her being a difficult child and not meant as a reflection on Miss Stagg! Miss Stagg resigned in 1922 and Miss Willis replaced her.

Other cases: a child of three caned on the hand and marked by a blow on the forehead by Assistant Macey, who admitted it and said it was on account of the child's 'constant dirty habits' (she got a reprimand); a complaint was made to the Superintendent that Miss Blundell of No. 1 Home had been consuming the jam and sugar and beating the children – complaint considered to be unfounded. Complaint by the father that his son was beaten with a broom and pushed up against a door, cutting his lip. That was put down to 'insubordination'. In 1920, an assistant, Mrs Pardy, resigned, 'having heard of the bad treatment of the children'. That same year, although he later denied having made the remark, Guardian Mr Nappiras commented that the children were 'starved, cruelly beaten and neglected, and the Superintendent is a brute'. The same year the County Medical Officer found that 27 of the children were verminous, many were also dirty, and their appearance unsatisfactory'. There can be no defence for this shameful regime, and no doubt that the charges made were well-founded.

Some fortunate children escaped from this miserable regime by being adopted. Apparently a process without formalities: a prospective parent would arrive, select a child, and leave with him or her. The lady quoted above who arrived at the Homes in 1911, recalls that a titled lady wished to adopt her sister; on being informed, presumably after consultation with the father, that the child was not available for adoption, the lady offered the father between £2,000 and £3,000 for her. This was such a fortune in those days, but it was refused – a moving tribute to a father who would not give up his daughters at any price, despite having had to place them in care through inability to support them.

For one and all in the workhouse Christmas was an occasion for indulgences and relief from the daily grind. They were able to enjoy not only the traditional Christmas dinner, with beer donated by Lord Malmesbury, but extra treats such as a carol service at the Priory, a lantern show or other various entertainments – a conjuror, a ventriloquist, a musical concert. The beer question was debated ad nauseum in the boardroom before each and every Christmas for about 25 years, always the subject of a resolution from Mrs Grimes, a fanatical temperance campaigner, and one who remained utterly convinced that most of the inmates could blame their woes on drink, and always she was defeated, usually heavily.

*Christmas 1905: the dining hall. Note the gas lights, bare brick walls and superb roof*

The children at the Cottage Homes had a Christmas tree from Lord Malmesbury each year, with gifts for each child underneath, prizes and toys.

Every year the Revd Bush (living in the former workhouse, of course, the Red House), would invite the adults to tea at the vicarage in spring; 1903 was the twentieth year in which he did so. There were other special occasions that the inmates could participate in: in 1902 it was the Coronation. Not all the Guardians took the same view of such indulgences: one, Mr Hutchings, wanted to give the inmates a piano concert and hire the piano. After Mr Druitt again objected to the inmates receiving a little of life's pleasures on the rates, Mr Hutchings generously went ahead with his plans, paying for it himself.

Annual frivolities such as this came to a sudden halt in 1914 with the outbreak of the first world war.

# Chapter Eleven

## War

No sooner did it seem that hostilities had commenced, then the Army arrived to assess Christchurch Workhouse for pressing into service as a military hospital.

The inspection in October 1914 proved satisfactory, and the following month witnessed the arrival of wounded Belgians to fill some of the 50 beds placed at their disposal in the old (original) infirmary. So began the vital and honourable role of the Red Cross Hospital in Christchurch which continued for the duration of the war.

All the staff with the exception of a night nurse were voluntary recruits – the 'VAD' (Voluntary Aided Department) nurses, from two detachments – 196 and 38 – under the efficient control of two lady 'Commandants', Mrs Louden, of Hengistbury House, Christchurch, and Miss Katherine Ricardo, of Bure Homage, Mudeford. These two redoubtable ladies immediately drew up a list of wants and energetically set about acquiring them. On the list, which was published regularly in *The Christchurch Times*, were pneumonia jackets, flannel bandages, blankets, cakes, cigarettes (Woodbines were especially appreciated; it seems incredible today that smoking was positively encouraged), soups, jellies, poultry and so on, a miscellaneous list that could include almost anything. A special band of lady egg collectors was even set up. Details of gifts received as a result of the appeals also went into the paper – no doubt to encourage a matching display of selfless generosity from those who would be embarrassed by their names never appearing as donors!

The Red Cross made many alterations to the infirmary to adapt it to its new use. They put in a larger kitchen range and installed gas heaters in the wards for hot water. There was also an operating room. New

*Red Cross nurses and Belgian soldier patients outside (original) infirmary*

# CHRISTCHURCH DOING ITS "BIT."

With the advent of thirty-five more wounded soldiers from the front our thoughts naturally turn to the Hospital which has been working at Fairmile since October last.

Through the kindness of the Guardians in allowing the removal of the cubicles, the Commandants have been able to open a new ward and thereby increased their accommodation to seventy-six beds.

This has not been done without considerable expense. The cots have been provided, but money is urgently required to fit the ward with lockers, tables and other equipment, and an earnest appeal is made for help in this direction. Of course the increased number of patients means also an increase in the current expenses. Such a small item as cigarettes, for instance, soon mounts up when one considers that from 350 to 400 are required daily—nearly 3,000 a week.

The expenses are reduced to the minimum. With the exception of one night sister the whole of the nursing staff, consisting of five trained nurses and forty other nurses and assistants, is entirely voluntary, as is also the medical and dental attendance, while a masseur attends three days a week at very much reduced fees.

The kitchen accommodation is very restricted for the amount of work which is required with so many to feed, and three wooden huts have had to be added for kitchen extension and storing kit, &c., while a gas cooker has been fitted, and rings also to each ward for use in the summer. To cook for 75 patients is no light work in a kitchen with a temperature which is a cross between a stoke hole and the equator. Those who stay at home should be prepared to give up something to provide those who are doing this work with the sinews of war.

The Quartermaster's duties are no sinecure either. She has to overhaul the clothes of the new arrivals and send them across to Fairmile House where they are disinfected without any expense to the Hospital. Here we might say that the Master and Matron of that Institution have rendered most valuable assistance in every way, and done much to increase the comfort of both the wounded and staff.

The Quartermaster has even a more difficult task when the men finally leave, as she has to requisition and see that they are fully equipped with everything for returning to their duties.

Now that the summer is coming on it has been found necessary to fit sun-blinds to the windows to keep the wards cool. The garden, though small, is greatly appreciated by the convalescents, who indulge in a quiet game of croquet. Any other out-of-door games would be much appreciated. If anyone can send any they would be doing a good turn for the men when time begins to hang rather heavily on their hands.

The Nurses and their assistants are always busy. The time which can be spared from their other duties is filled in with darning and repairing clothes, no inconsiderable item with 75 men whose mending is some months in arrears.

Mention must also be made of the stretcher bearers who have given a good deal of time and assistance in not only bringing the men from the railway station, but, in helping in bathing those who are unable to do so unaided. Also for carrying patients from the operating room back to their wards after the operations.

With the stretcher bearers those may be coupled who have come, often at a moment's notice, with their motor cars for the conveyance of the wounded to the hospital.

A great amount of work has been done, but it must be realised by all that there is still a greater amount to do, and each one in his own circle must do his bit. It is not necessary to go farther afield to find a sphere of usefulness.

It is recognised that there are other urgent calls—but let us continue to do this one thing well first.

*The Christchurch Times 15 May 1915*

wards were added, utilising buildings that the Guardians has used for other purposes, increasing the hospital's capacity to 80 beds. These opened in October 1915, 'spacious and lofty buildings of wood and corrugated iron, with brickwork chimneys', reported the local paper. Each of the two wards was 66' by 25', lit by electricity, with bathrooms and lavatories attached. They were christened the 'South Africa' and 'New Zealand' wards. Names of the Empire were used for all the wards at the time – others were Malta, French etc. There was also a Kitchener and a Haig ward. The opening of one of these wards is illustrated nearby: it appears to be Lady Malmesbury doing the honours – she was President of the Hampshire Red Cross and

*South Africa ward*

used the ancestral home, Hurn Court, as a convalescent hospital for the soldiers. The photograph was taken in the boardroom.

*Opening a new Red Cross ward: Lady Malmesbury officiating*

Soon afterwards, a strange addition was also grafted on – a boathouse lent by one Mrs Scott, which was used as a recreation room. New appeals went out to equip it with furniture and games. Mrs Scott may be the individual referred to in a letter to the writer from Ruth, daughter of Guardian F E Abbott, as possibly a doctor's wife 'and was up at Fairmile overseeing the VADs during the first world war. She was known as 'Sister Scott' – a large, muscular "Dragon" who put the fear of God into all the nurses!'

The Commandants had under their direction various Medical Officers, forty Red Cross nurses, Quarter-Masters, a housekeeper (Mrs Alan Druitt), four cooks and ten kitchen helpers. A 'Stretcher Company' was based at 15 High Street, the Druitt home (James Druitt had died by 1904) and currently the library; this was commanded by Major Gardner, with a Mr Lord second-in-command, and Herbert Druitt as secretary.

The Guardians felt the loss of their old infirmary keenly, but got it back in its extended state in January 1917, having been obliged to hand over their larger and brand new infirmary to the Red Cross, so great was the need. The men were being sent from the trenches by sea to Southampton and from there to Christchurch by train, where they were met by volunteer 'ambulance' drivers in their own cars who brought them up to the hospital. Such was the continued need that by April of that year, the Guardians were faced with a request from the HQ of Southern Command to hand over the entire workhouse for the sick and injured soldiers. They did not do so, but a year further on handed back the old infirmary to the Red Cross, so that both infirmaries were now requisitioned. Where the inmates were moved to is not recorded, but it is probable that out-relief was more generally given. The Red Cross had begun its work at Christchurch with 50 wounded soldiers; by the time the Armistice was signed they had 300.

Whilst this account provides the bare bones of these events, a moving insight into the work that was done by Christchurch people to aid the soldier-victims of the battlefields has been left to us, a tribute that provides a remarkable record of one who was on the receiving end of the marvellous work that was done there. Some anonymous but gifted writer sent a series of articles to *The Christchurch Times* in 1918. It is reproduced below almost in its entirety, both as a unique, detailed, first-hand account of the Red Cross hospital, and to ensure that those who contributed to its success will have their efforts once again recorded eighty-odd years after its first appearance in the local paper.

## A HOSPITAL TRIBUTE

### We Come to Christchurch
### By "Malta"

*The twin screws wildly thrashed the water for a moment or two, we heard the scraping rattle of the anchor chain sliding out, and then Chippy said quietly from the next bed, 'Thank Gawd, that's Bloighty'. As the boat's bow came round, the sun shot a column of light through the one porthole by which he could peep in - 'Jerry's' malevolence had closed the rest - and used the dancing waves as reflectors to make his welcome more evident still. And we were soon to see him, for the orderlies quickly hoisted us up from the ward to the deck. There, in the clean sunshine and clean, bracing air with its sea tang, we had our first sight of England as we lay in ordered rows on the stretchers awaiting our transfer from the train. Beneath the cloud-flecked sky, the wheeling gulls screamed their welcome, the honest whistle of a passing engine shrilled to the same key, and the strong sea wind whispered it to us as we lay there silently, joyfully, expectant. And it was with this chorus of welcome that Blighty began the cure of her sons broken in the wars.*

*The quick, competent, nonchalant orderlies soon switched us off the boat and onto a stretcher carriage into the ambulance train, where the padre was waiting to take air wires to the home folk, to distribute stamped postcards, or to obtain newspapers, whilst in the shed was a girl waiting to do her bit with a supply of sweets and a very obvious willingness to do any old job for us, from the posting of letters onwards. And as we lay waiting for the train to start we wondered idly . . . whether these offices of welcome would continue for long, whether we should leave them all behind us at the port.*

*A whistle from the engine, and we began to glide along an English railway and see English placards, and be stared at by English eyes set in English faces; but our destination was still in the lap of the gods . . . Then came a very smart, button-polished, chin-shaven sergeant, who passed along from stretcher to stretcher with the detachment of a professional providence and informed us all whither we were bound. 'Umpteen, you're for Christchurch,' was the remark he tossed to me. But it left me cold, for Christchurch was nothing but a name, its excellencies were still to be found, and it needs but a very short military experience to rob one of all sense of responsibility . . . Soon, the engine began to slow down, and curiosity was awakened as to Christchurch: what sort of a place it was, how we were to be treated, was food strictly rationed, and were the hospital rules reasonable. As the train stopped, we saw on the platform civilians, armed with stretchers and with a look of nervous anticipation on their faces; we did not know that they were real amateurs, lovers of their work. The 'walking cases' were soon out of the train and off to the hospital, whilst we 'more unfortunates' were left in helpless, curious uncertainty. In came the first two stretcher-bearers and were directed to their patient 'number so-and-so', but their nervousness was still as evident as their willingness . . . the nervousness was lest by any kind of awkwardness we might be caused an unnecessary twinge of pain. The bearers could not realise that we should have thanked them if they had caught us by the legs and arms and dropped us on the stretchers, for how can those at home know what Blighty is, and all that it means to us? And we too did not at first realise what it was to shed our numbers and become men whose need was tenderness, gentleness, and utter kindness. Orderlies would have unloaded us with the swift, heartless efficiency we knew so well, but we were receiving the treatment accorded to sick friends who had come home. And all the little nervous mistakes only made us more certain we had come back too, and deepened our consciousness of the atmosphere of absolute kindliness that pervaded the whole platform.*

*. . . Cigarettes came in a shower, and those, too, of the right sort . . . Were we smoking, then it would soon be finished, and if we hadn't one, the want must be immediately supplied. The slightest draught stealing gently through the door produced an extra blanket, and the need of a match meant the gift of a box. We had shed our numbers and become honoured guests, treated with the lavish hospitality that comes naturally from the right kind of Englishman, a type surely indigenous in hospital.*

*Our welcome had exceeded all our expectations; in its kindly forethought, it almost transcended our belief, but gave us an assurance that while we had been 'over the water', those left behind us had neither forgotten not forsaken us.*

## We Arrive at the Hospital

*'Well, boys, you are awfully lucky to get to Christchurch,' remarked one stretcher-bearer as we 'more unfortunates' lay helpless on our orderly stretchers in the waiting room. We made no response, but puffed away stolidly on our cigarettes . . . But Christchurch as yet was nothing but a 'place'. . . . It had been pointed out to us on a map, and it was merely a little round black dot with a name tagged on it . . . Consequently, all remarks about the place fell upon uninterested ears. We were in 'Blighty', and that was a far as we could comprehend.*

*It was a 'Blighty' sky we could see through the windows, English men were running around, intelligible advertisements hung on the walls; 'Blighty' was about us everywhere, so how could we*

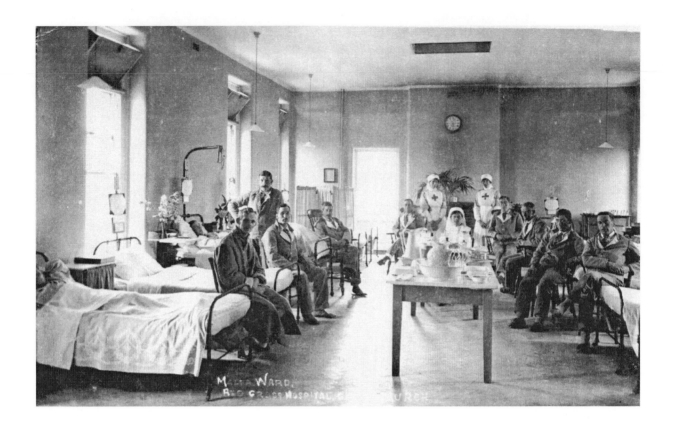

feel interested in Christchurch? . . . Therefore, no enthusiasm was aroused. The Christchurch hospital might be 'the best in the South of England', but we know that a little actual experience was worth a considerable deal of puffery. 'It's a VAD hospital, you know'. That, admittedly was worth knowing. 'The building's quite new, too,' added another, and then, as an afterthought, 'and it's run entirely by ladies'. We thought we might quite like Christchurch, an opinion that was confirmed by a gentleman by the door who remarked with unction and appreciation, 'Yes, boys, and they're all pretty,' . . . The time had at last come for us to be loaded up, and we went to the top storey of the ambulance and started off. But the spring had got into the veins of that driver, the exhilaration that can only come with the feeling that one is doing good, had fevered her blood, so quickly he switched us out of the station, shot us over the bridge, whisked along Fairmile, and sent our hearts into our mouths with the turn into the hospital, jerking them safely back again as she drew up at the door. With a strong steady pull, we emerged from the ambulance hood, were carried past the polished doors with their immaculate brass, and set down in the entrance hall. Why is it that entrance halls of all hospitals bid you to abandon hope? . . . There was a bareness, a chill, a loneliness about the hall that depressed us . . .

'Malta' was the ward to which we were assigned , and up the stairs we went, 'specials', as it were on the landing to guard us and ensure our safe ascent. But on reaching our destination a feeling of great and final contentment was ours . . . We looked round about, and everywhere the blatant efficiency characteristic of the military hospital was camouflaged, swamped, hidden beneath that dainty lure of colour which is the distinctive note of the right kind of woman. The chill, white patternless counterpanes of the military hospitals were gone, and in their places a bright-patterned *pink, spotlessly, but not obtrusively, clean, and the screen too did not stand up in utter nakedness, but their white wooden frames were draped with the same pink fabric that hid the untidiness of many of the lockers, and there were flowers too: some daffodils nodded their golden trumpets to one, whilst from the other side stole the delicate fragrance of the wild violet. In short, wherever one's eye lighted were obvious signs of the deft dainty hands of our womenfolk who have no peers the wide world over. But the last few words of an article are not sufficient to devote to our nurses.*

## An Inside View

*. . . In the morning light . . . you become more sure of things. For in the cold, clear light of the dawn you see things as they are, and then you know it was no dream but a glorious reality. You actually feel sure that you are Home, that the nurses are real and substantial, that 'bully biscuits' are not on the menu, that we are in hospital, in a VAD hospital, where there are neither early 'revallys' nor absurd or ridiculous rules. Then you turn over, prepared thoroughly to make the most of your good luck . . .*

*At the head of the whole hospital are the two Commandants, and only one of these two is known to us in 'Malta'. Now, the 'Commandant' suggests a grim, austere, bespectacled madam who says to this one 'Go' and he goeth, glad of the chance, and another 'Come' and shiveringly beneath her cold stern eye he cometh, and to another 'Do this', and he hops quick and doeth it tout-de-guile. That notion is the very antithesis, her spirit informs it, the men's utter contentment is the best testimonial to her efforts . . . And the Sisters in their sphere are like unto the Commandants. They listen to our tale of woe yet never look bored, nay, rather interested in the whole thing. At first it seems a bit strange to have a Sister who greets you with a smile and encourages you with a joke, is obviously interested in some jape you are tempted to retell for her benefit . . . And what can one say of the Nurses? That they are all beyond compare? But that of course goes without saying. One hears of the Waacs and the Wrens and the Land Girls breeched and legginged, their photographs are the mainstay of the Pictorial Press, but in the quiet wards of the hospital of the land, girls are doing work about which there is no glamour, and around which the limelight never plays. But that does not mean that it is unappreciated. We who gain by their work will never forget. The war will become a memory, the hospital a photograph, and Christchurch lapse again into a black dot with a tag on it, but the kindnesses of which we have been the recipients have been so indelibly impressed on our minds that they can never 'pass into nothingness'. And the great glory of the place is that the spirit is so widespread. It is no wise confined to this or that nurse, but is common to all. In fact, the only contention that one can imagine between the nurses is as to which of them shall show the greatest kindness and consideration to the patients temporarily in their charge . . .*

The consequences of the war for the Guardians went far beyond the loss of the two infirmaries. The call-up meant that the dreaded able-bodied young men were very thin on the ground (and very thin). We may expect the Guardians to have been delighted, but in fact they depended on workhouse labour to maintain the premises, especially their extensive grounds. The 28-30 acres were by then 'practically useless'. The Guardians considered this difficulty, and then came up with their usual answer – a committee.

Whatever the committee's solution was, it plainly did not work, as the War Agricultural Committee severely criticised the Board for the state of the land. The ground had indeed been sown, but the crops were lost through subsequent neglect, and this was in 1917, a time of acute food shortages. By the middle of 1918 the Guardians were seeking assistance with the cultivation from the soldiers at Christchurch Barracks.

Rations were reduced in 1917 and the waste of bread was to be treated as a breach of discipline. The average weekly consumption of meat was 1lb per head, and of bread, 6lb per head. On two days each week

KITCHENER WARD, XMAS. 1918

a pint of oatmeal (gruel) was substituted for 4oz of bread, though some inmates refused to eat it. Sugar was also in extremely short supply.

By April that year, the Government asked for the bread ration to be halved and substituted by flaked maize and oatmeal (strange echoes of the Corn Law-induced bread shortages of 1800).

The casuals who swamped the wards each weekend (their numbers also swelled by the closure of casual wards at Lymington, Poole, Ringwood and Lyndhurst) were an especial problem, in that the physical work they were required to do used up excess bread supplies. They had a pint of oatmeal for breakfast and 8oz of bread with 2oz of cheese at dinner; by the following year they had to manage on precisely half this quantity of bread and cheese. The general workhouse diet in that year, 1918, was gravely inadequate. All that was provided in the infirmary seemed to be a thin slice of bread at breakfast, a herring for dinner and porridge for tea – the patients lay awake all night with hunger. The Guardians discussed this: Mr Crawshaw made the extraordinary assertion that he would welcome some of the substitutes himself, but they did agree to add 2oz of bread to the tea and breakfast. The Master could not get suet for puddings; boiled rice was substituted. He had plenty of sprats, he said, but no oil to fry them in. In the end, there was not even any cheese for the casuals.

The herrings on offer left much to be desired: a supply had been obtained that had been intended for export to Germany before the outbreak of war four years previously. German POWs had refused to eat them. A Guardian, Mr Baker, relayed the story to the Board and exhibited a sample, holding it aloft amidst much laughter. They were, he said, fit only for manure. Not all thought so: a Mr Beaton claimed to have tried them himself and found them 'very good to eat'. The proposal to destroy them was defeated.

In other respects, workhouse life went on as before. Christmas 1915 was celebrated as usual: 'The large dining hall at Fairmile House on Christmas Day', said *The Christchurch Times*, 'certainly did not give those present the idea of a seething mass of discontented humanity.' There was roast pork and beef, cabbage, potatoes, plum pudding, mineral waters and coffee, tobacco and snuff, apples and oranges. The soldiers had their own festivities, including competitions for the best decorated ward. Kitchener won it in 1916, with an elaborate ceiling design of falling snow devised from the cotton wool supplies (used or yet to be used? Obviously not rationed!).

'Seething discontent' was nevertheless as evident amongst the casuals as ever – the majority of whom were described by the Master as old and decrepit men. One woman ran away in workhouse clothing and was given six weeks' hard labour in prison. A man who had worked in the morning on his allotted task refused to scrub the kitchen floor after dinner, saying it was three men's work. It may well have been. He was half-starved, he said, and could get no employment. No sympathy was given him by the magistrates. Colonel Brander told him there was plenty of work for able-bodied men like him, and sentenced him to a month's hard labour.

The Cottage Homes were a fertile recruiting ground for the army and navy, of course: almost 50% of the boys joined up on leaving and the news of their progress was relayed to Board meetings. There were times of sadness when the news was bad, but also times of pride when one did well for himself. A welcome letter arrived from an ex-Cottage Homes boy, now a man, who had joined up 18 years before as a drummer boy and had climbed the ranks to Sargeant-Major. He had, he said, 'fond recollections of Mr Found, and also of Mr Macklin, his schoolteacher'.

Those whose destiny lay in a life at sea also kept in touch. One reassured the Guardians that press reports of unkind treatment on the training ships were incorrect. Only about one in every 200 men got flogged each week!

At the Homes themselves, then still under the strict Blakeborough regime, the problems continued as before the war. In 1918 two girls absconded because their hair was cut short on account of ringworm – a frequent problem at the Homes – and five boys later also ran away. The birch was used for punishment, but in this case the culprits were sent to an Industrial School. Miss Stagg was again accused of physical maltreatment of other girls by them in 1919; this time she was warned by the Visiting Committee that they would not overlook further episodes.

When the war petered out in 1918, the Guardians put on record their appreciation of the dedicated services provided by the Red Cross hospital. They got their infirmaries back, disinfected and cleaned. The soldiers lingered on in the town: quoting Ruth Abbott again, she recalled that some had been shell-shocked and others had trench foot, but were soon sent back to the Front. 'Some came back after the war and came to Shortwood (the Abbott home in Magdalen Lane), destitute and begging – our maids always gave them their food and my mother gave them money. How badly we treated our heroic men. I saw this in both wars.'

Mrs Louden received the OBE for her Red Cross work during the war. She became President of the local Red Cross Society which operated from her home at Hengistbury House, loaning medical equipment to the poor. A Red Cross ambulance was begun in 1931, and the Society worked to raise awareness in hygiene, sanitation, infant welfare and tuberculosis. She died in 1939, just as a new European war was breaking out.

# British Red Cross Society.

## CHRISTCHURCH V.A.D.     No. 38 and 196, HANTS.

\*   \*   \*   \*   \*

**VICE-PRESIDENT:**

THE COUNTESS OF MALMESBURY, Heron Court, Christchurch.

**COMMANDANTS:**

MISS K. RICARDO, Bure Homage, Christchurch.

MRS. LOUDON, Hengistbury House, Christchurch.

**HON. TREASURER:**

MR. H. W. PAUL, R.N., Stanpit House, Christchurch.

THE Hospital was opened on the 29th October, 1914, when fifty wounded Belgian Soldiers were received straight from the battlefield. The Commandants beg leave to express their grateful thanks to the following, viz. :—

The Subscribers who have so kindly and generously contributed to the Guarantee Fund.

The donors of clothes, papers, vegetables, &c., for the use of the patients.

The members of the local Ambulance Corps who have voluntarily attended at night to bathe the patients and who have also cleaned boots and uniforms.

The Local Hairdressers' Association, who have shaved the patients gratuitously.

The ladies and gentlemen who are lending their motors to take patients and nurses about.

They would also like to take this opportunity to explain that should it not be found necessary to expend all the money guaranteed, the remainder will be returned to the guarantors, with proportionate reductions.

*(DRO RHM collection)*

# Chapter Twelve

## On to the next war

The end of the first world war found the Guardians extremely busy making up for lost time. So much had had to be deferred, on account of the Red Cross, the price and unavailability of building materials, the shortage of labour, and so on. Projects that had had to wait included the two extra Cottage Homes, the mortuary and the tramps' wards. These were to go ahead, but the first new building was to be an extension to the nurses' home which was completed 1925 and filled most of the area between the existing home and the boardroom. (A further extension in 1933 joined the two buildings up.)

Then there was to be a new infirmary for the women. This was completed by 1924 on land to the rear of the site, and is now known as G Block. The open-air shelters were added in 1925.

Almost as soon as it was built, the infirmary was taxed to its utmost, reflecting the slowly increasing medical, rather than economic or social role of the workhouse. The entire block was therefore extended to the south to house another 44 beds in 1929. The work was done by the firm of Bryant and Trowbridge at a cost of £13,500, and the top floor was reserved for maternity cases. The Master, now Mr Morgan, spoke of this achievement in his half-yearly report in 1930: 'undoubtably one of the best of its kind in the country.

*Women's infirmary extension under construction*

*Women's infirmary*

*Ward in women's infirmary*

Bright, cheerful and comfortable, its balcony will prove a splendid acquisition in fine weather,' he reported. He went on to reveal that three side wards on the middle floor would be used as nurses' bedrooms pending the future extension of the nurses' home. The shelters, which are largely intact, were used for TB cases. TB was rife through the 19th and 20th centuries until its spread was halted by the development of antibiotics in the 1950s, and it was common practice to keep patients in the outdoor shelters all year round.

*The Bournemouth Daily Echo* in April 1925 gave an account of an investigation by a special sub-committee of the Guardians into casual ward provision and standards. They reported to the Board that their enquiries had shown that no changes were necessary. The beds, said the casual inmates interviewed, were clean and comfortable, they were supplied with literature, and two unsuspecting representatives of this roaming class of rootless types were even questioned by a 'plain-clothes' Guardian in King's Park. Both these men said that Fairmile had the best casual wards they had come across. On learning of these investigations, Guardian Mr Winter became concerned that conditions were so good that a rush of casuals could be expected from all over the country – the tramps had an uncannily effective grapevine, and his words turned out to be prophetic. Another comment which revealed much about the reputation of Fairmile House amongst the travelling community was from Mr Kemp Welch, who said that years ago the institution had been nicknamed 'the feather-bed workhouse'. It certainly seems to have reinforced that reputation from these latest innovations – but what a far cry from the cold contempt in which this class of person had been regarded less than half a century before. Yet a visitor in 1926 was 'distressed to see so many men herded together and wished something could be done to give them more freedom on Sundays.' The Master pointed out that he was bound by the Casual Order of 1925 in the conditions in which the tramps were kept.

*Wash stand in vagrants' ward*

*The Elizabeth Wood rest rooms*

Their diet at this time consisted of a breakfast of a pint of tea with 8oz of bread and an ounce of margarine. Dinner was 8oz of bread again, an ounce of margarine as at breakfast, 2oz of cheese and some potatoes. This was the diet laid down by the Ministry for Health; there was never any meat, much to the concern of Guardian Mr Peaty.

In 1928 the tramps' wards (as the casuals were now more generally known) were extended at a cost of £3,211. A new humanity was being demonstrated in their design: the cell system was done away with in favour of 'rooms resembling miniature hospital wards, lighted by airy glass skylights above', reported *The Christchurch Times*. The brick walls were lined with plaster, central heating was installed, a drying room for their clothes, three baths and a water spray, washing sinks and even a day room for their food rations: 'The minimum necessary for cleanliness and comfort which they have a right to expect from a Christianised society,' commented the paper. Such sentiments were echoed by Mrs Shave in her election address that year: 'Much of late has been done to give more light, air and colour to our buildings and to impart a greater aspect of warmth and cheerfulness to the whole institution.' Kindness, in fact, was overflowing almost to surfeit. One Elizabeth Wood, of Walpole Road in Bournemouth, left the sum of £2,000 in her will of 1926 to provide day rooms for those aged women 'whose circumstances and age necessitate the care and attention of the Guardians of the Poor'. The result was the semi-circular-bayed, single-storey, cottage-type structure which was built on the Fairmile Road side of the original infirmary. A newspaper reference to it soon after described it as 'special, well-furnished rooms for ten of the best-behaved and most agreeable women inmates'.

The flurry of building work was also necessitated by the continually rapid growth of Bournemouth. The population of the Union had reached 104,068 in 1925 – it will be recalled that in 1901 it was 69,339 – and 90% of them lived in Bournemouth. The overwhelming preponderance of Bournemouth inmates forced a name change on the Guardians, or rather, permitted the representatives of that town to push it through. From that year, the Union became the Bournemouth and Christchurch Union, much to the fury of the Christchurch Guardians who naturally took great exception to their town's name coming second in the title, having been the originating parish back in 1764. The seal of the old Board was acquired by Herbert Druitt, but as with so much that he painstakingly saved for posterity, its current whereabouts are unknown, if it still exists at all. The front cover reproduces an impression of this seal.

Another long-delayed project was a new mortuary. This was also built in 1928, replacing one that had to make way for the new women's infirmary.

This period saw the last of many Guardians who had been serving the Board for considerable chunks of their lives. John Kemp Welch had given 45 years, 21 of them as chairman; Mr Kitcher 30 years, also chairman for many years; Mrs Grimes, now also a JP, had been 27 years on the Board by 1927. Another long-serving lady member, Mrs Alice Shave, died in 1932. Her obituary in *The Christchurch Times* referred to the 'steady fire of perpetual kindness' she showed whilst undertaking her 'gracious work of inestimable worth.' Typically, she left provision in her will for income to be paid to the poor and needy on a regular basis. She was, incidentally, the aunt who brought up Mr Ken Smith, well-known in the town for decades as the Congregational Church organist, Chamber of Trade president, and mayor.

A new broom was sweeping through the boardroom, and it was being pushed hardest by Bournemouth Guardian Mr Tom Peaty, who was a very new sort of animal – the red-hot socialist. He claimed to be the only representative of the poor on the Board, although his assertion received this sniffy comment in our faithful loyal paper's editorial: 'From our experience [the Guardians'] primary duty has always been to to relieve the necessitous poor.' But Mr Peaty was the genuine article. The traditional beer-for-Christmas debate received short shrift from him: 'It was not', he said, 'beer which was to blame so much for bringing about the downfall of men and women, but it was the environment of the latter which led them to abuse it. They did not hear all these tirades against the wealthy class when they indulged in intoxicants.' The beer had been donated for the occasion by Mr W Hale, a Guardian.

By 1926 the number of nurses had risen to 26, and to 33 by 1930, although resignations remained a problem. A Medical Officer, Dr Lyster, suggested rather provocatively that some of them found conditions intolerable.

*The Board of Guardians, late 1920s. Back row: 2nd from left, Councillor Taylor; 4th from left, Tom Peaty; 5th from left, Councillor Little. Front row: 2nd from left, Mrs Grimes, then Mrs Morgan (Matron). Extreme right: Miss Blandford*

Mr Blandford, the Relieving Officer for the last 37 years, retired in 1926. It was estimated that in that time he had covered 60,000 miles in the course of his work. By bicycle. His replacement was Mr A H Smart.

Another change at the workhouse was the arrival of a new Master and Matron, Mr and Mrs William 'Bill' Morgan. 'He came to Christchurch in 1920 with a great reputation', said a Guardian, Mr Tunnard, 'which he has maintained ever since he was appointed.' One of his first initiatives was to plant trees along the Fairmile Road frontage. Mr Morgan became President of the National Association of Poor Law Officers and was also an examiner for the Poor Law Examinations Board.

During the twenties and thirties, the porter and his wife were Mr and Mrs Esterling. They brought their daughter, Charlotte, to live with them at the porter's lodge, and this lady was able to remember those days with great clarity. The late Master and Matron, Mr and Mrs Crockett, whilst kind enough in their own way, she recalled, were constrained by the Guardians from making any unnecessary expenditure. They were, therefore, unable to improve the lot of the inmates, whose standard of living was very basic.

The arrival of Mr and Mrs Morgan made a vast difference in this respect, as they managed to add the hitherto unheard of luxuries of jam and cake and milk to the spartan diet of bread and margarine. Mrs Esterling was particularly compassionate in her role of assistant matron and then cook. Charlotte remembered how her mother would take advantage of Mr Morgan's absences at the sailing club to rustle up extra supplies of cakes for the inmates.

There was also still a workhouse uniform for the women – grey dresses and a white apron and cap. It was, apparently, most unattractive, but the new Master did away with it and allowed the women to wear pretty coloured dresses – still made in the workhouse, but much less of a 'pauper's' outfit. One day per month was permitted as leave of absence, for which occasion the inmates were given their own clothes back. The innate goodness of some of the workhouse officials is demonstrated by Mrs Esterling's habit of giving such inmates

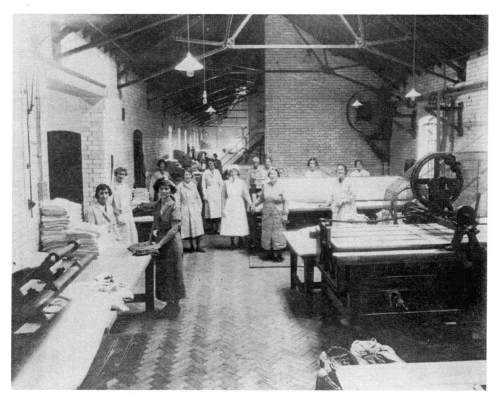

*The laundry: female inmates in print overalls*

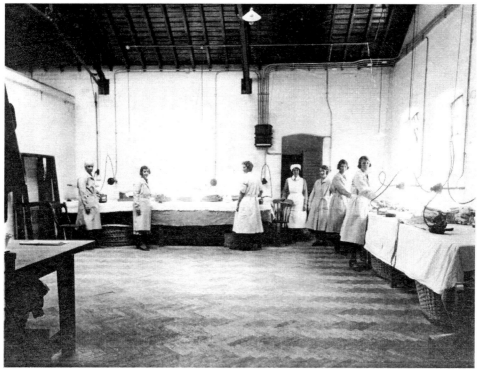

*The (gas) ironing room*

*Kitchen c.1920*

half a crown out of her own pocket for their lunch. One of the nursing staff, Lucy Jefferson, was made from the same mould. She was Superintendent Nurse for some 30 years (and can be seen in the front of the Master's House with the Morgans on page 69). Described by Mrs Luckham (the former Charlotte Esterling) as in some ways eccentric, given to dramatic tantrums, she specialised in making coconut ice for the patients when well-disposed. She died soon after retiring in a domestic gas accident. The picture, kindly loaned by Mrs Luckham, is a rare photograph c.late 1920s from the workhouse era. In the centre foreground are Mrs and Mr Esterling; behind them are some of the casuals, roped in on vegetable-peeling duties, or suchlike. They are making rice puddings. Note the lady with the cat – no restrictive Health and Safety legislation then! She was Miss Margaret Seward, who later married an inmate, Eddie Pearson. Between the Esterlings is George Faulkner, and behind Mr Esterling a former actor, then 'Vic', then Mr Groves.

More changes were afoot in the wider local government area: the ancient post of Overseer of the Poor, initiated five years before, was abolished in 1927. Although their functions had recently been reduced to preparing assessment lists and collecting rates, their previous functions had included the burial of the dead thrown up by the sea, the issue of beer-house licences, the prosecution of 'rogues and vagabonds', the prosecution of those who kept 'disorderly houses', the preparation of jury lists, and, of course, the relief of the poor.

In fact, the overseers were the earliest form of local government, out of which the Guardians of the Poor had evolved. They in turn were now facing extinction.

The number of inmates had risen to 441 in 1926, partly on account of the General Strike. The good reputation of Fairmile House was widely appreciated by would-be inmates from outside the Union 'trying to wangle their way in' (Public Assistance Committee, 1933) which was prevented by the Settlement Acts still being enforceable. Incredibly, people appeared to be killing themselves because they could *not* get in, as

*Men's infirmary from the rear*

opposed to the contrary situation in earlier periods when two people committed suicide rather than have to enter the workhouse. In 1927 a man of 80 who had sold his cottage and was all ready to go into Fairmile House, actually did do away with himself when he learned that he was to be sent to Fordingbridge instead.

Those who did benefit from the care they received in the infirmaries would sometimes thank the authorities. One such patient wrote that it was 'more comfortable here than in expensive sanatoria'; another said that, 'I should feel condemned if I did not put on record all the kindness that has been shown to me at Fairmile House. I went there 14 weeks ago in an almost dying condition. Besides all the skilled attention, there were the little kindnesses, and the wireless added to my happiness and kept me in touch with the outside world.' This was installed in 1928, the funds having been raised by public subscription and the balance made up by Captain H B Norton. Captain Norton was a regular benefactor, from a fortune made in India. Each Christmas he gave 2s 6d to each inmate and tea and sugar to the women, 'baccy' to the men, sweets for the children. He also donated the clock tower in Bournemouth Square, now topping the new camera obscura.

Christmas was still celebrated in style, the inmates 'for a few hours living again as though the world had treated them fairly' (*The Christchurch Times*). Mrs Charlotte Luckham recalled that preparations for Christmas began weeks in advance, when the decorations for all the wards were made. In 1926 100 inmates were taken on an outing to the New Forest in a 'Royal Blue' charabanc; one old lady, taken there by private car, had not been outside Fairmile House for seven years. Christmas 1927 saw the nurses carrying lanterns through the wards and singing carols at midnight. That year the Priory choir visited the wards and other parts of the House. Such public-spiritness was typical of the age.

Unemployment in the twenties was high, and the Guardians attempted from 1920 to alleviate it when they could by giving the building work to unemployed men. Some worked on excavating the site for the women's infirmary, others were employed in the ornamental grounds and gardens, perhaps on the tennis courts that were laid out next to the newest infirmary.

New consideration was given to the 'lunatics', now more kindly referred to as mental patients. Knowle County Asylum was still used, also the Park Prewett Mental Home in Basingstoke. As with all categories of inmate, their numbers increased, despite the passing of the Mental Deficiency Act in 1913 which was meant to relieve the Guardians of this responsibility. In 1920, three such people were maintained by Fairmile House in these and other such institutions; eight years later the figure was 18. Still, a report from the mental hospitals was encouraging: no more strait jackets and their own cinema and concerts, with cricket and football for the men.

The veil of time preventing us from peering inside the House was partially lifted in 1927 through an article written 'by one who has been there' and published in *The Christchurch Times*:

*It is questionable if 90% of the pedestrians and others who daily pass the Poor Law institution ever permit themselves to wonder . . . how the inmates spend their lives. By a good many people a pauper is regarded with feelings akin to repulsion rather than a subject for commiseration . . .*

*Some years ago, the Board of Guardians throughout the country, in an effort to remove the stigma of pauperism, abolished the term 'workhouse' and substituted a more euphonious name for their respective asylums. True, a distasteful appellation has fallen into disuse, but –*

*"You may break, you may shatter the vase if you will,*
*But the scent of the roses will hang round it still."*

*. . . The institution under notice is commodious, scrupulously clean and distinctly hygienic in every way. Mr William E Morgan is the competent head of the establishment, and his efforts for the welfare and comfort of those under his supervision are ably seconded by the Matron (Mrs Morgan) and other officers, whose popularity, created by their untiring anxiety for the well-being of those under their care, is as genuine as it is general . . .*

*The food* [the inmates] *are supplied with is wholesome, and not a few able-bodied men, and women too, could emulate 'Oliver Twist'. But when one considers that the work they have to perform daily (those who are capable of undertaking any) could not by any stretch of the imagination be styled arduous - in reality it is only exercise - the diet is quite ample.*

*What hurts the bulk of the inmates . . . is the confinement. True, they are allowed certain liberty and their relatives and friends are permitted to visit them weekly, yet the privilege of freedom . . . is curtailed, and this rankles in most of them.*

*Even some of the old men, particularly during the summer months, take their discharge periodically in order to feel that the shackles of restraint no longer bind them . . . On the other hand, there are some inmates who very rarely, if ever, go outside the walls, and this habit breeds a very uneven, cantankerous temperament, and as often as not they are soon ostracised by their former chums.*

*The effects produced by an environment associated with a workhouse cannot honestly be said . . . to be conducive to health, especially during the summer months when the inmates are prevented from rambling through the grounds and enjoying the fresh air . . .*

*Moreover, to not a few of the inmates the penned-up process is distinctly detrimental to their well-being. With some of them, melancholia* [depression] *is engendered, and, try as they may, they are incapable of shaking it off, and eventually become anything but normal. The tempers of others become deranged, irritability forming one of the conspicuous phases of their character.*

*Some of the men and women are sub-normal when admitted to the House, while others develop strong mannerisms as a sequel to constant worry . . . Continually, one sees faces which suggest fretfulness, a sullen revolt against life and circumstances and fate . . . To the inmates who had decent jobs prior to the Great War and now find themselves cooped up in this fashion, the position is, to say the least of it, certainly nerve-racking.*

*Of the inmates at present in the institution there is a good percentage of able-bodied men who ought, in the ordinary course of events, to be working hard at some useful occupation outside; while on the other hand, there are incapacitated old men . . . who are simply awaiting the arrival of the Grim Reaper.*

*The majority of the men lead an empty, uneventful life, and although the soul-degrading restrictions and humiliations of the bad old days are practically evils of the past (the Poor Law system having greatly changed for the better . . .), there is still room for improvement with regard to liberty, the innovation of more useful work for the inmates, and reading facilities. Under the circumstances, however, the general body of inmates ought to be thankful . . . that such an institution is in existence.*

*Notwithstanding the fact that the Poor Law is an admirable one, there are several distressing features about it. For instance, when a man leaves a Union institution . . . he is in exactly the same predicament as he was in when he entered the House - 'broke' financially, still without a situation and . . . shabbily attired . . . To turn a man adrift without money, in poor clothes, and with no employment to go to, certainly retards rather than facilitates his restart in life.*

This suggests that the dreadful tasks of stone-breaking and oakum-picking may have come to an end before this time, probably during the first world war, something confirmed by Mrs Luckham 's memories, as she could not recall any such work being done in her time. A picture of food shortages, confinement and boredom is conjured up, the women working in the laundry and the men, including the vagrants, in the garden or on the land. Crops were still being grown in the extensive area behind the Cottage Homes and on the workhouse land in the region of the present-day MacMillan Unit.

The article also illustrates the lack of employment, despite Labour Exchanges having been set up in 1909.

The workhouse system was about to be abolished. But the Bournemouth and Christchurch Guardians had no intention of making a quiet exit after an existence of nigh on 100 years. The Poor Law was not being reformed, they said, just being transferred to a new body, the Public Assistance Board. The transfer would be costly and the change was a result of 'a craze for centralisation'. Nationally, the same concerns were being voiced by the Poor Law Unions Association, whose President's final address condemned the 'closing down of such a large body of voluntary effort' as 'a spiritual loss to the nation' and 'a national catastrophe'.

One of the failings of the system was that the new pensions for the elderly and widows were inadequate, and relief was still needed by them. In 1925, there were 187 people over the age of 70 in the Union on relief; the majority, 100, were in the House. Three years further on, the new Old Age (Contributory) Pensions Act was passed, allowing those over 65 to receive the pension, yet only three people out of 156 then in receipt of poor relief came off it as a result. Record numbers of people continued to be admitted; nationally, in 1928 the Poor Law institutions and hospitals housed more inmates than in 1915, despite the pensions and 'the Minister's statement that these institutions are emptying,' said the clerk. The increase in the old-age pension to 10s a week was simply insufficient to maintain them.

The Boards of Guardians were to be abolished on 31 March 1930. Agreement was reached on the management of Fairmile House. Christchurch was hived off from Bournemouth – the final insult – so the long link going right back to the formation of the Union in 1835 was severed. Instead, Christchurch was to come under the jurisdiction of Hampshire County Council. Local people were most concerned that their relatives would not be allowed use of the infirmaries, but instead would be compelled to travel to Ringwood or Fordingbridge, but a stay of execution in this respect of five years was given. The Christchurch inmates were, of course, in a minority by then. Figures show that on average in recent years only 55 locals were in Fairmile House and only ten in the Cottage Homes, all the rest being residents of Bournemouth.

It was thus the County Borough of Bournemouth which was awarded 'custody', as it were, in this tug of love (or power). The Bournemouth town councillors toured the institution a few days in advance of the changeover, and the newspaper account of this event records their surprise at seeing wards filled with flowers, cushioned chairs, rosy curtains; there was a well-equipped nursery apparently brim-full with toys, and the infirmary patients were kept occupied (by choice, at this stage of the workhouse history) with activities such as sewing.

The Bournemouth County Borough created a Public Assistance Committee and a Guardians' Committee, the function of which was to advise the Public Assistance Committee on relief matters. Members of these committees included Councillor Gelsthorpe, Mr Kitcher and Mrs Grimes. In a valedictory article, *The Christchurch Times* applauded the Board with the following tribute: 'Fairmile House has earned for itself a splendid reputation … the best-equipped institution of its kind in the country … The Guardians have shown kind and humane consideration … for the poor and infirm … excellent work in the relief of suffering … Many of them have their hearts in it so much that they are truly sorry for the change.'

There was one Guardian slightly sceptical. Mr Peaty's response to all this adulation was that 'he could not help feeling that evidence should be given by the men who had been in the wards and could give facts relating to the difficulties they were up against.'

The number of tramps using the casual wards during the inter-war period escalated dramatically during this depressed time and led to a headline in *The Christchurch Times* in 1930 of: 'Nearly 10,000 Tramps a year!'. The article following went on to chart the rise, which had soared from 952 in 1920 to 9,544 in the last year – a tenfold increase.

By 1938, meat was appearing on the menu for the casuals for the first time, but a seaman who complained that it was tainted and discoloured and therefore threw it away, was punished with 14 days' imprisonment, despite the Master acknowledging that it was indeed inedible. An enraged individual signing himself 'A Christchurch Provision Dealer' wrote to the local paper with the observation that the transgressor 'will be offered better food in any prison in the country than he obtained at Fairmile House' – further evidence of the low standard of the diet. Other casuals tried to bring their own food in: this was also a punishable offence.

Punishments remained severe. A Swiss man, resident in this country for 27 years, was recommended for deportation by the magistrates after a fight with an attendant, in addition to receiving a sentence of 28 days for the assault and 14 days for 'refractory conduct'.

## The Cottage Homes

The overcrowding was relieved by the opening of two new Homes (numbers 5 and 6) delayed by the war, in 1926. At the start of the war, about 150 children had been crammed into accommodation designed for half that number, so the extra space was badly needed. Each one cost £4,000: 'Everyone was delighted with the spick and span appearance,' enthused *The Christchurch Times*. One Home, Number 6, was to be pressed into service as a nursery for the under-fives under the auspices of a 'specially trained official', Miss Perks. No expense was spared, apparently, in providing the new young residents with all they needed by way of dolls and other toys and pictures.

Some children could be boarded out still, but only if orphaned or deserted. On lucky boy was adopted by his foster-parents. Foster parents were paid, which caused some resentment among local families who had to raise their own children on far less. Others went as before, to Canada or Australia, a practice which in recent years has been the subject of books and TV documentaries revealing dreadful abuses and misery caused by an ill-thought-out and badly monitored social experiment.

Life for the children went on as usual, with the occasional treat, for instance one arranged by the Bournemouth Rotary Club to the Theatre Royal. May Day was another occasion much was made of; once the children were even permitted across the road to the boardroom to show the Guardians their fancy dress. The Cottage Homes Girl Guide troop was invited to Highcliffe Castle to meet Queen Mary in 1928. Christmas continued to be very special for them, and one occasion when they would eat with real enthusiasm. In 1926 the 84 children apparently got through 600 oranges, a hundredweight of pork, 20 dozen mince pies and 300 other cakes in two days. The Homes were decorated with imagination: one had a winter scene recreated in the hall with Red Riding Hood and the wolf in bed and the dayroom decorated as fairyland. Another Home in that year, 1929, featured a Woodland Wedding tableau with intricate details, such as a miniature illuminated church. The boys' Home featured a realistic fantasy garden complete with water-lilies and flowerbeds. In the old schoolroom, a huge Christmas tree, donated as always by Lord Malmesbury, was covered in gifts.

*Cottage Home No. 5*

# CHRISTCHURCH UNION.

### Superintendent of the Cottage Homes
### September, 1922.

Admissions since 30th Sept., 1921 ... Total 61

Discharged to present date ... ... 62

Discharged as follows :—

| | |
|---|---:|
| To relations ... ... ... | 24 |
| Boarded out ... ... ... | 12 |
| By removal orders to other Unions ... | 3 |
| Boys and Girls—Domestic service in hotels, &c. | 5 |
| Infirmary—all made a good recovery ... | 6 |
| To Sanitary Hospital—scarlet fever, ditto | 4 |
| Special Homes for mentally deficient children | 3 |
| ,, Industrial Schools ... | 1 |
| ,, T.S. Mercury for Royal Navy | 1 |
| ,, By adoption ... ... | 1 |
| Emigrated to Canada (boys) ... ... | 2 |
| No deaths ... ... | - |
| | Total 62 |

1872 children have been dealt with at the Homes since 15th May, 1901 during the service of the present Supt. and Matron, Mr. and Mrs. Blakeborough, and during the whole period of 21 years and 4 months not a single child has died at the Homes.

During the same period 1766 children have been discharged to relations and service, and quite 96 per cent. have done well and are now leading the lives of respectable citizenship, and less than a dozen have died including five who died fighting for their country during the Great War. Sixty old boys joined His Majesty's services during the War and there was not a single conscript amongst them.

One old boy, now at Brixham, has got a full Captain's seamanship certificate and controlled a mines trawler in the Mediterranean during the war, and two boys are Warrant Officers in the Navy.

The Scouts—3 patrols of 8 (total 24) have been well maintained during the past year.

Girl Guides and Brownies (24) have been established during the past 12 months under Miss Froud and Miss Horrell, and these organisations have had a splendid effect on the present good tone and discipline at the Homes.

Corporal punishment during the past year has been almost nil and so the good conduct all round has been a credit to our children and the staff. And the health of the children has been very good and illnesses rare for the past 21 years.

R. BLAKEBOROUGH.

*11th September,* 1922.

*Cottage Homes Report, 1922*

*Cottage Home Christmas decorations*

*Priory School: Cottage Homes children identifiable by the girls' cropped hair, square-yoked smocks and laced-up boots; boys in sailor-type jackets*

In 1929, Clarendon Road School was opened, an event which led the Guardians into a furious confrontation with the Education Authority, which refused admission to Cottage Homes children (on grounds of space). Little children as young as five or six were having to walk down into the town to attend the Priory School – four times a day, as they came back for lunch, so it seemed only sensible and fair to allow them to attend the new and closer school. Indeed, in the words once again of *The Christchurch Times*, the Authority appeared to have 'barred, bolted and fortified' the school doors against them. The Guardians were both courageous and defiant, even at one stage in the argument prepared to take direct action by taking the infants to the new school and challenging it to expel them. Eventually, in the face of the Guardians' valiant campaign in the final weeks of their existence, the Education Authority gave way and allowed a measly ten places for the infants.

The Blakeboroughs retired from the Cottage Homes in 1932 amidst tributes aplenty from the members of the now defunct Board of Guardians. 95% of the children turned out well, said Mr Kitcher, and many of the ex-Cottage Homers returned to visit to show off their new spouses and babies.

In the place of the Blakeboroughs came Mr Harry Dunn as Superintendent and his wife, Elizabeth, as Matron. Mr Dunn organised sports days every year on the Cottage Homes green. They were to be the last holders of these posts.

## Memories of Cottage Homes Inmates

Not many people who grew up in the Cottage Homes are willing to talk about those days. Their memories are of being jeered at in the school playground, of wearing identical clothing, of not having parents and not knowing normal family life. Fortunately, one lady was prepared to speak out and the following is based on her account. This was the situation when the first edition of this book was published; it brought to light

*Mr and Mrs Dunn*

further contributions from other former workhouse children, which as the reader will soon learn, comprise a picture entirely at odds with the cosy descriptions which went before regarding Christmas jollities and other rare enjoyments. But, to continue with our original account:

This lady arrived at the Homes in the early twenties, her parents being alive but unable to support her or her brothers and sisters. Her father was in Fairmile House, and she was able to visit him there once a week (so the original restriction on children visiting the workhouse must have been lifted), but had no contact with her mother. Conscious though she was of her poverty, she was nevertheless aware that she was better off in the Homes than the children of the Pound Lane or Pit Site slums in the town.

She remembers the interiors of the Homes – the polished vitreous flooring, the forms in the dining hall, the plain but nutritious food. She left at the outbreak of the second world war, but still remembered the unvarying meal routine of soup and fruit pudding on Mondays, fish on Tuesdays, roast meat on Wednesdays, soup and an orange on Thursdays, suet puddings on Friday and a roast again on Sundays. Saturday meals are not recalled.

Each child had a number, and this was on their pegs and sewn into all their clothes. She remembered wearing ribbed stockings, button boots, serge dresses and pinnies, but also remembered that Mrs Dunn very quickly made improvements to the girls' clothing after she arrived in 1932, arranging for them to wear prettier dresses, which they greatly appreciated. Ten children slept in each dormitory, which had a spyhole in the door. Outside were extensive grounds, cultivated by workhouse labour from Fairmile House, and the piggeries. The children used the old schoolroom as a hall; it had a stage that they used for plays and other activities such as Girl Guides. The shoemaker had a workshop in another part of the school. The lady who was the Guide leader was one of the kinder adults to come into contact with the Cottage Homes children – Miss Froud, of the well-known local shop family.

The children largely made their own fun. The excursions, such as they were, consisted of an annual trip on the tram to Bournemouth to see the 'pictures' – incredibly, it was always the same film – Scrooge, ironically. Her memories of other officials were not so warm: the Blakeboroughs were hard in their dealings with the children, as perhaps was to be expected of those whose values were formed in the Victorian age. The Dunns were kinder; Mrs Dunn in particular being a warm-hearted person. Mr Peaty, the fiery socialist, was remembered with amusement as the Guardian who instructed the young children not to stand for the National Anthem; as this went against the orders of the other Guardians, much confusion arose. Discipline was strict, and the children were treated rather impersonally – there were simply too many of them, she recalled, for individual attention to be given. Years later, when in service in Christchurch, she glimpsed her employers cradling their new baby in their arms by the fireside, and realised with a pang what she had missed out on in her formative years.

Discipline sometimes involved cruelty – physical punishment. One poor girl who accidentally wet her bed was beaten with a batten of wood. On this occasion, she had the courage to bring the incident to the attention of the Guardians when they visited and ritually went through the process of enquiring of the children if they had any complaints; the assistant concerned was dismissed as a result. It was this strength of spirit that enabled some children like this lady to come through this institutional upbringing relatively unscathed. Others were far more affected emotionally, and some of the girls were sexually molested at the Homes by staff, her evidence showed, a very serious allegation but one supported by other sources.

During the same period, a small boy came into the Cottage Homes and had similar memories. He especially remembered the concrete yard between the Home and the wash-house which had to be scrubbed down each and every day by the boys. His Home, No. 2, had a typical layout of kitchen and dining rooms downstairs, with a store for boots and shoes, and the dormitory upstairs. The wash-house outside also featured a coal-house and latrines.

The grounds were tended by workhouse labour, and included a kitchen garden on the site of the present Queensmead rest home. At the rear of the land was the piggery; every week one was killed on the site and carted over, draped with a bloodied cover, to the workhouse kitchen opposite.

The schoolroom housed the dentist, the gardener (Mr Seymour ) and the shoemaker (Mr Hopkins), and was used as a schoolroom during the second world war only, as an overspill on account of evacuees.

He had a brother and a sister in the Homes, but as they were brought up separately, the usual policy being to separate siblings, he grew estranged from them. Today, this is rightly regarded as being most harmful to a child; how much worse in situations where the parents are also out of contact for one reason or another. School was at Clarendon Road, where the Cottage Homes children were invariably blamed for any misdeeds. The uniform was blue or grey trousers and jersey, and a red and black tie.

One day, this small boy played truant from school. Not knowing where to go to escape detection in his tell-tale uniform, he sat down in despair at the side of the road in Fairmile, next to the milestone (boundary stone, more likely). As his hands touched the ground, he was surprised and delighted to feel them touch a coin: the grand sum of tuppence. He rushed down to the '2/6 store' (Woolworths) in the town to purchase a rare treat of a sweet. With his prize in his hands, he sought cover by a haystack at Latch Farm. Alas, when he opened his treat, he discovered to his dismay that all he had obtained was a packet of cream crackers. He ate them, dry as they were, all the same.

His most abiding memory, and most profound regret for his childhood, was never having had a goodnight kiss, emotionally deprived as such children became.

The extracts below are taken directly from letters received in response to the first edition, punctuated and spelt as they were: First, from a man born in 1927:

> *I will not talk against Mrs C-, but she was a very hard Auntie* [the style the assistant matrons came to call themselves], *I went through <u>hell</u>. No one knows how the boys at that time and years went through, every elder boy had to look after a younger one, besides doing his own job, mine was to scrub the courtyard every morning before breakfast and it had to be clean, after all had to line up for school, my twin brother was in the next House, we used to meet outside the gate and share our money if we had any that is, we did our level best to get 2½ p between 4 of the boys then on the way to school go into the bakers, at the back + buy a large loaf which I used to take into the classroom & put into my my desk until 1st bell, then in the playground tear it into chunks between us, you see we were always hungry, never enough food to fill our bellys, dinner time we had to go back to the Homes, a long walk, after back to school, evening walk back home again, oh my my, after meals it was my job to clean all the boots, 23 pairs off them, what a rotten job, every day then off to bed.*

> *Weekends I had to work, take the bread around to the houses then help Mr Hopkins the cobbler or Mr Seymour the Gardener, I did not mind that, I learnt how to mend shoes . . .*

> *One winter going and coming from school, it was cold, very cold, my feet were like ice, with me were two other boys, Gandhi & Whisky, nicknames, well Whiskey was very small, his feet were very very small & he could not walk. He was crying with the cold, so I got him on my back & walked home, it took a long time, well we all three got indoors, the Auntie was waiting for us, her name was Laidlaw, she got hold of me & said, where have you been? I told her the ins and outs about Whisky, called me a liar, said I had been playing, no I said, with that she smacked my face 3-4 times up the Hallway then down again, you have been in the park, no I said again, she beat me so bad I did not know what too say, then, all of a sudden a voice in my head, tell her you have been on the swings & she will not hit you any more; so I said yes, I was sent to bed, no tea that day . . .*

> *When I was 8 years old [1935] my Mother died, she was only across the road, I did not know until* [name omitted] *my step-father came and told us Mummys dead, sad day. Now on to when I was 16. You had to leave the Homes, they got you a job, always put on the farms . . .what a life!! had my clothes taken from me every night so I could not run away, I did in the end, well then I was put into the workhouse at Fairmile Rd, oh dear, what a life living with the old boys, see them pass away, I did not understand, I soon did . . .*

The next account comes from a man born in 1925, one of three boys together at the Homes, but, as usual, separated in different buildings:

*As I recall we were always hungry, which led us as a group to such escapades as robbing orchards . . . stealing free samples of such things as dog biscuits, or dried chocolate drink mixtures from doorsteps and scrounging left overs from 'outsiders' as we referred to other ordinary kids at school. We would also make hasty searches of dust bins for sandwiches or any other tasty goodies discarded by our more fortunate fellow students.*

*Our diet at the time consisted largely of oatmeal porridge seasoned with salt (never sugar) and a slice of bread and dripping, plus a large cup of unsweetened coffee. We all returned from school at lunch times for a hot 'dinner', usually consisting of poor stew or rabbit or sometimes fish, but with lots of vegetables cooked English fashion until the guts had been boiled out of them. Naturally we would get through the meaty portion first and then dawdle over the hated vegetables, and because time to get back to school (about a mile away) was limited, often the unheated, inedible vegetables would be saved for the non-eaters evening meal. That usually consisted of 2 slices (thick) of bread and margarine with either jam or cake (never both, however). If you happened to be one of the non-veggy eaters like me, you had to eat the cold dinner left-overs (they even marked your name on the plate) before you had any tea. Failure to eat the leftovers meant you simply had nothing else to eat all evening and went to bed hungry. Can you wonder that we were perpetually hungry, stooping literally at times to eating things we found in the street or the gutter. . .*

*[Of about 1935] Now can you imagine that of, say, 35 boys, a halfway dozen regularly wet the bed. This caused quite a chore, drying out mattresses, washing bed linen & night shirts every day. So in an attempt to curb this, the culprits . . . were deprived of water & liquids during meals and the morning their bed-wetting crime was discovered they were forced to stand in a corner of the large stone-floored entrance hall, dressed only in their night shirts, with nothing on their feet, with the wet portion of the sheet held up to their faces, regardless of the time of year . . .*

*Most of our spare time was taken up by completion of allotted chores - peeling potatoes and preparing vegetables for the following day, washing current days dishes, wash clothes (shirts, socks, towels and similar items) mending them such as sewing on buttons. . . darning socks . . . cleaning shoes, cleaning windows, swabbing cold stone floors, polishing wood floors, brushing carpets . . . During school days this had to be done in the evenings, seven days a week, excepting those days we had other mandatory activities, such as boy scouts meetings, first aid classes, band practices . . . Although we went to [a] public school, we rarely if ever got involved with extra activities, such as sports or theatricals, choir or school band* [because of the expense involved and the obligation to do the chores].

*Writing this, I now wonder just what it was the 'nurses' actually did. We did all the cleaning, inside and out, made beds, washed dishes, prepared vegetables, looked after our 'younguns', did most of the repairing of clothing, cleaned boots, supervised our 'younguns' morning and evening teeth cleaning, face washing etc, made our charges beds and cleaned up after them . . . When necessary the older boys also cleaned out all ovens, fire grates and flues by hand. In addition, daily, all toilets, wash basins, bath and bathroom floors and washroom floors had to be scrubbed. Then put in a full day at school. We became identified more by our 'Homes' number than by our name . . . no name, just a number.*

*Clothes: we always wore leather boots, laced at the ankles, with thick grey woollen socks that reached the underside of the knees . . . we all wore shorts all the year round and had no under garments. We had grey flannel shirts buttoned up to the neck with attached collars. During the* winter we had woollen pullovers and a darker grey coloured jacket. But I recall being cold . . . Covering our heads up was a cap with a small peak in the front, grey coloured. For rainy weather we had a 'sou-wests' a black oil skin that turned up at the front and reached well over the back of the collar to prevent the rain from running down the back of the neck. What ever the season, whatever the weather, we were recognizable for who we were and thus easily avoided.

Recreation: On rare occasions . . . the good burgers of Christchurch and/or Bournemouth would do good things on our behalf. I well recall around 1932 or 1933 being taken on a 'cavalcade' by a group of men with cars; being packed into the 'rumble' seat and being driven around Christchurch for hours and the whole group periodically stopping for sweets and ice cream and all sorts of soft drinks on this hot summers day . . . These kindly men were magical in their largesse and promised us they would make it an annual affair. Sadly for us that was the only time they did it, but I always treasured it as a magical day. Sometime during the late '30s several of us senior boys were taken to a place somewhere quite close to Christchurch where we saw some sort of historical pageant when the

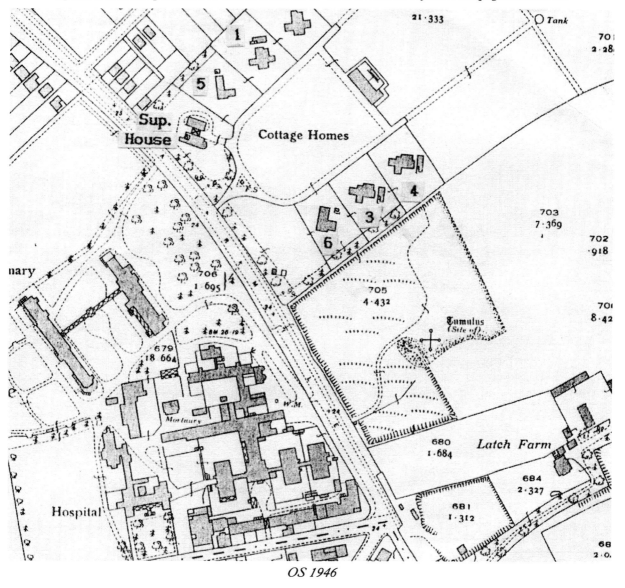

OS 1946

*participants were clothed in Regency-type costumes* [Bure Homage, 1935: Frank Ricardo's fundraising event.] [The carnivals are recalled next.] *Each year we went to Boy Scouts camp for 2 weeks. This, for us, was a revelation because for that brief spell we knew what it was like to eat normal food - eggs and bacon, toast and marmalade, and over-sweet tea for breakfast; stews and other filling fare for lunch and a typical meat and potatoes followed by dessert for dinner . . .* [Meeting his mother in the dining hall of the workhouse] *All of us would gather there and sit in little clusters, the nearest thing we had to privacy. The mothers (I never recall seeing a father there, ever!) often fed us a cake, dessert of some kind or another . . .*

*Punishment: Except for attending school our contacts with 'outsiders' was little if any, although when gangs from our groups massed to do mischief, such as raid orchards . . . such barbarous acts inevitably led to violent responses, especially for those less fleet of foot. And we had no one to comfort us, admissions to anyone in authority would result in further physical assault upon each of us.*

*Punishments* [included] *a cane* [from the Master]; *punishment within the Homes was less clinical, it could be with the bare hands or the dreaded cane and/or be in the form of extra work allotment, deprived of meals, forbidden to go out . . . Such punishments were frequent and liberal for all of us.*

## Memories of a Cottage Homes 'Auntie'

Miss W Coffin was put in charge of Home No. 2 at the young age of 22 in 1936, although she had memories of the Homes going back to the mid-twenties. At that time, she recalled her grandmother, who was employed there, taking 'direct action' against Mr Blakeborough by snapping the cane that he was about to use on an offending boy. Food during those days was strictly no frills: thick bread doorstops with mugs of cocoa were the staple diet. The arrival of Mr and Mrs Dunn brought a softer regime. One of the first changes was the exchange of boots for shoes.

Foster-mother was the new name for 'matron', and they were known to the children as 'Auntie'. The foster-mothers had a great deal of autonomy, and so the atmosphere of each Home very much depended on the Auntie's character and methods. For instance, Miss Coffin went to some trouble to prepare something tasty from the meat allowance; in other Homes it would simply be placed in the oven to cook as it was.

The boys still had a uniform of sorts, consisting of a grey shirt with navy and red tie and a cap to match with red cord, worn with trousers of varying colour. In the summer they wore khaki-coloured shorts with shirts of various colours. The girls did not appear to have identical clothes.

Many of the children came from seriously deprived backgrounds and some were very sad cases. They were better off in the Cottage Homes than with their families, and also better off than being boarded out, as this was often only done for financial gain. More than forty years after the Cottage Homes were closed, Miss Coffin still received correspondence and visits from the men who grew up in her Home; proof that some of the children from the period had reason to feel real affection for the place of their upbringing and for the staff who had done their best to give them a secure and happy childhood.

# Chapter Thirteen

## The NHS

It was apparent that another war was on its way. VAD nurses were once again at Fairmile House, now a Poor Law Institution, practising air-raid drills on the green in the centre of the Cottage Homes. Miss Hamilton was a Commandant and a Miss Beech-Johnston her assistant, together with a Lady-Superintendent, Miss Heriot-Hill. They also erected a hospital ward in the schoolhouse, all of which activity received hearty commendation from the visiting War Office inspector, Major Newland.

Once war broke out, Fairmile House was once again pressed into service to help wounded soldiers. This time the injuries referred to did not seem on quite the dramatic scale as in the first world war: instead of trench foot, patients had a variety of minor disorders, some very odd indeed, such as the patient with a 'hysterical' shoulder. There is an account of these times from one of the soldiers treated there, from which we learn that two wards were used by the Emergency Hospital (in the Women's Infirmary), mainly for army patients, who relished being away from the military discipline usually a feature of army hospitals. So much, it would appear, that high spirits would erupt into pillow fights and the like, which the appearance of one Sister Burnett usually quelled. The soldier-patient remembers the lovely grounds, immaculately kept and complete with a bowling green. The Cottage Homes played a role too in the war, receiving children evacuated from Southampton.

Life for the inmates went on as before, it would seem, though concerts and suchlike had become rather scarce. Christmas was still made much of, both here and at the Homes, and the mayors of both Christchurch and Bournemouth would attend to help serve the food to the inmates, who numbered about 450 (excluding the Cottage Homes) in 1944.

It seems that the old people at Christchurch were still having to go to Fordingbridge, as one old lady wrote to *The Christchurch Times* about the difficulties this was creating for relatives and friends wishing to visit them. Christchurch Council was also pressing for this to be changed – it was a consequence of Fairmile House being run by Bournemouth Council since the abolition of the Guardians in 1930. The day seemed to have been won by 1949.

*Soldiers and friends at Emergency Hospital*

It was after the war that Fairmile House faced the next major upheaval, and it was one that was resisted by local people just as fiercely as the Guardians resisted the 1930 upheaval. This was, of course, the creation of the Welfare State in 1948, and the transformation of the institution into a hospital.

On 15 July of that year, the entire Poor Law was abolished. Out went the Public Assistance Board, in came the National Assistance Board. Poor Law relief became National Assistance, which was a state and not a local provision. Swept away with it was the whole paraphernalia of settlement rules, and contributions from relatives for those being maintained in Poor Law institutions and the removal of pensions for the same purpose from inmates receiving them. Not that the Guardians of the old days had entirely disappeared from the scene: Mr Peaty and another Bournemouth ex-Guardian, Mrs Saye, served on the Welfare Committee of Bournemouth Council and thus continued to play a part in the developing hospital.

A Regional Hospital Board was created, but administered for a while by the Fairmile Agency Committee, the job of which was to wind up the previous Public Assistance Committee and lead into the Hospital Management Committee. Bureaucracy still flourished.

The first act of the new Board was to attempt to transfer all the aged people, so inconveniently using beds that now had 'hospital' labels on them, out to St Leonard's Hospital, originally a wartime hospital for the American air force, near Ringwood. This move did not endear the new authority to the people of Christchurch and Bournemouth. Even the old Poor Law officers railed against the plan: 'It would seem', wrote Mr Morgan, so recently Master of Fairmile House, 'the planners under the despised Poor Law had bigger hearts and more enterprise than those with the "new look".' A Bournemouth councillor, Mr Owen Ellum, joined in vociferously, praising Fairmile House as 'a splendid building, well-managed and … the envy of all local authorities. The inmates look happy, well fed and well housed … Some of the people have been there a very long time … and they regard it as a happy home.' He called a public meeting, where Mr Peaty accused the Hospital Board of the 'utmost cruelty' in their desire to move the old people out, and paid tribute to Mr Morgan who, he said, would have prevented the loss of Fairmile House to the hospital service had he still been the Master (Mr and Mrs Foxall had taken over from him two years before the NHS was created). 'The powers-that-be', he claimed, 'would never have been able to manipulate things as they did and try to make out that the major use of Fairmile House was for sick people.' Joining in the fray, a Mr Cogswell stirringly reminded his audience that: 'Are not some of these people the sturdy old folk of England, who raised their families without any assistance from the State? Their children were raised without any free milk or schools and without family allowances. Perhaps if they had had some of these things, they would not be where they are now.'

Christchurch Council joined in the protests, as did the patients, who organised a petition to the King and Queen and the Prime Minister, Mr Churchill. A member of the Regional Hospital Board accused the organisers of forging the signatures! The local Labour Party also took up the issue and wrote in support to the Ministry of Health.

The beds were needed so that the Hospital Board could add surgical facilities. The battle against this 'medicalising' of Fairmile House was fought hard. Mr Morgan referred to previous attempts to grab the best wards, 'to oust those for whom they were designed and built, and the attempts were made just because the old Board of Guardians had made such a good job of them.' Surgical cases had always gone to Boscombe – the Royal Victoria Hospital (demolished c.1992). It had been a voluntary hospital. This arrangement left Fairmile House with the chronically sick and infirm, and it was this position that the objectors sought to maintain. Mr Peaty was again in the forefront of opposition, supporting Mr Morgan's view that 'the medical facility have had their eye on [Fairmile House] for many years.'

Aneurin Bevan himself replied for the Ministry of Health. He declined to meet a planned deputation and backed the Hospital Board. All looked quite hopeless, but out of the blue in 1949 the Fairmile Protest Committee, as they had styled themselves, was advised by the Ministry that the scheme was being abandoned indefinitely because of – the Ministry claimed – capital expenditure cutbacks. It was never revived, but the Hospital Board found another place in which to decant the elderly …

After the opposition was subdued, Fairmile Hospital, as it was now titled, became the focus of an intensive programme of refurbishment and expansion. The training school for nurses, in the old original lying-in ward next to the infirmary, expanded and built up an excellent reputation. It was in 1949 the first school of its kind in the county, and grew from nine trainee nurses in 1951 to 92 pupils and three teachers in 1967.

The first prize-giving of 1951 achieved a 100% pass rate. Apart from an intake of students from the UK, there were girls coming over from the Continent and Australia. By 1954 there were about 70 nurses sleeping in the nurses' home. The accommodation for them was constantly being improved and modernised, the 'old Poor Law furniture' being dispensed with in 1956 and a new nurses' home opened in 1964. This was named Trinidad House in recognition of all the Commonwealth nurses who were trained at Christchurch Hospital, and opened by Sir Learie Constantine, the West Indies cricketer. So good became the training school's reputation, that by the 1960s the General Nursing Council used it as a model for visitors from overseas to study before returning to their home countries to set up similar establishments.

By 1954, an article in *The Christchurch Times* described the hospital as having 'modern and comprehensive equipment' but no operating facility or out-patients' department, apart from physiotherapy. A children's ward had developed, and by a quirk of fate had been put in the very same building which the children from the first workhouse had come to in 1886. At the time of the NHS takeover, there was some sort of nursery, as Bournemouth Council's Children's Committee minutes refer to a provision for the under-threes, especially those 'deprived of a normal life'. When Poole General Hospital opened in 1969, the children's unit was closed down and the children transferred there, whereupon the old school/children's accommodation was converted to a Day Hospital for the elderly (with a typically hideous, unsympathetic and vast NHS front extension).

The Grand Plan for equipping Christchurch Hospital as a General Hospital was unveiled in 1955, and involved a scheme to the tune of £577,000 to provide a surgical operating theatre in G Block. This was duly opened in 1957 by the Mayor of Christchurch, Councillor Ken Smith, who was also the nephew of Guardian Mrs Alice Shave, as previously mentioned, and by the Bournemouth Mayor, Councillor Templeman. Echoes of the past were also invoked with the arrival of Red Cross ladies on the wards, though now they were distributing confectionery and magazines instead of bandages and Woodbines.

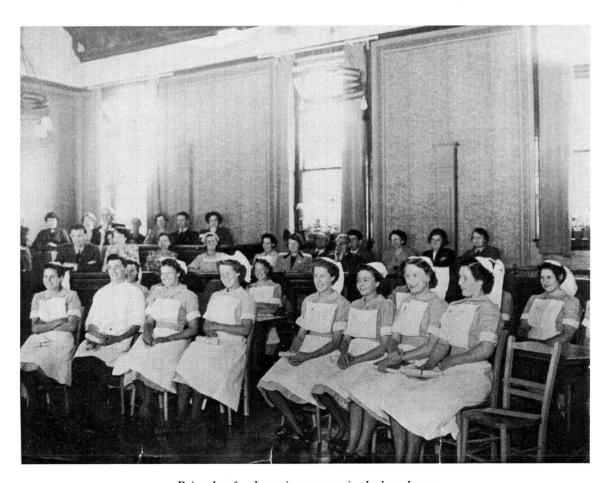

*Prize day for the trainee nurses, in the boardroom*

By 1961, the old inmates' dining hall had been converted to a staff canteen, with the usual tasteless NHS insult to better designers of the past – in the case, the great Christopher Crabbe Creeke – of a polystyrene-panelled false ceiling hiding the intricate barley-twist struts spanning the lofty beamed roof, and the even more glorious stained glass windows (see rear cover) which as a condescending gesture were permitted to be glimpsed once the self-service bar had been reached – when the attention would most likely have been drawn downwards rather than upwards. The kitchens were upgraded, H Block (male infirmary) modernised to include central heating, new bathrooms, and floors (so out went the lovely maple-block flooring of 1913), and the laundry once again extended and modernised. Incredibly, one inmate remained throughout these transformations: Miss Nellie Farnham, aged 77, who had been admitted way back in 1924, in the days of the Board of Guardians and when it was still the Christchurch Union. Thirty-five years later, Miss Farnham, who had rheumatoid arthritis, said: 'The hospital has changed very little. There have been redecorations, new beds and furniture, but apart from the new surgical unit, the main buildings have remained much the same.' She felt that hospital life today was rather more 'official' than in the old days, but 'there is still a personal touch about the place'.

The redecoration to which Miss Farnham referred was described in the ever-watchful local paper as 'quite unlike the severe black, white and olive green "barracks" of a decade ago [i.e. during the war] but now glowing with subdued pastels, bedspreads of pink, peach and green, nurses' outfits in light mauve with white aprons, and green tunics for male nurses; Sisters have dark blue with white aprons, Matron has maroon.' The children's unit, it went on to say, had 'French grey on one wall, peach and beige on another; others are turquoise and honeysuckle …' So much for the taste of the fifties – it must have made the children feel even more sick to gaze on the colour scheme.

*Christmas 1956: staff include Matron Miss Lewy (extreme left); Mr Horace Scott, chairman of the House Committee, behind; Cllr Ken Smith left of centre. Behind him is hospital secretary Mr Geoffrey Guy. Centre front: Sister Bennett*

*The 'floral corridor': this was alongside the dining hall and dated from the workhouse era (courtesy The Nursing Mirror, 1953)*

The hospital grounds soon found more buildings springing up in place of the ornamental grounds, notably the John Farmer school for the mentally handicapped, alongside the old children's school etc in Jumpers Road (1959).

Once the old people had been moved on – the story of this follows at the end of the chapter – there remained only one more problem in the way of the new hospital's up-to-date image, and that was the tramps. They were annoying many people by then, by clambering through the hedge by the nurses' home, which they appeared to regard as a short cut, by disturbing local residents and even those across the road in the Cottage Homes, with their drunken behaviour at night (they were meant to be inside between 9pm and 5am, but the hospital authority was ineffective in this respect, unlike their predecessor Guardians, who well knew how to impose order on vagrants). They damaged property and offended with bad language. Female tramps would turn up and be turned away, since it had become the policy at some stage to admit only men.

Each day, between 30 and 70 tramps would turn up at the 'Reception Centre' – the post-NHS euphemism for the casual wards. Mr Morgan encapsulated the new situation in a speech to a local Conservative Association

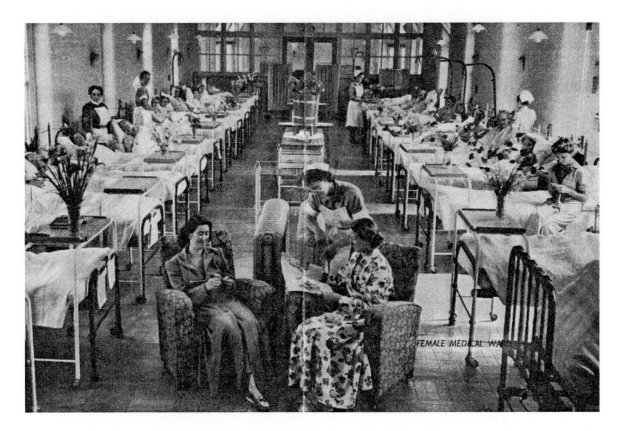

*The Female Medical Ward (G Block today) in 1953 (courtesy The Nursing Mirror)*
*(compare with the same ward illustrated on p. 114)*

in 1951: 'Lots of things have been said about the Poor Law, but one thing it did was to ensure that anyone in need did receive assistance, and it did ensure that idleness was not encouraged. If wayfarers took advantage of the accommodation, they were required to do a job of work unless they could show that they had work to go to. Under this new Act ... the position is that vagrants can frequent institutions and need not be required to do a job of work. Everything is made easy for them.'

Certainly, what work was required of them was a whole lot easier – maybe some cleaning, some gardening, washing dishes or vegetables, or, at worst, some wood-chopping. Not that the usual refusals were not heard and duly met with short prison sentences. Mr Ken Smith, then a magistrate, said that on the first offence all that was done was to reprimand the recalcitrant tramp. So different from the summary justice of seven days' hard labour as of yore.

In 1956, the Christchurch Hospital Management Committee said in their report: 'We have had enough of the Reception Centre, but realise the people who occupy it have a rightful place in the world.' It was decided that this rightful place was at Hurn, to a 'spike' as such places were nicknamed by the travelling fraternity, after the device used for oakum-picking. This was somewhere in Matchams Lane, which Hurn Parish Council valiantly offered for an initial three-year period.

So, by 1967, there was but one vestige of workhouse days – one small stretch of chocolate-brown corridor.

After all this fever of activity, it seems incredible that the Ministry of Health should have sought to downgrade the hospital – now a general hospital – to a geriatric unit. Massive public opposition was once again mustered: 10,000 signatures were collected on a petition organised by the Christchurch Hospital League of Friends (established in 1954) and once again a deputation was refused, this time by Minister Kenneth Robinson. He dismissed the campaign as 'emotional'. Writing in *The Christchurch Times*, journalist

Jack Dwyer pointed out that 'our hospital is the well-balanced, happy organism it is BECAUSE it has so many departments.' Once again, the campaigners proved victorious.

## Last of the Cottage Homes

As soon as the NHS took over the Poor Law Institution in 1948, Bournemouth Council directed their attention to the Cottage Homes. This was not a predatory move, but a response to the changing way in which the care of children was being regarded. It was no longer considered to be in the best interests of such children to be raised in an institution – but that is only part of the story, the official line.

All seemed to carry on as before, except that there was no longer a Superintendent. Mr Dunn had died at the young age of 49, nine years into the job. He had done much for the children, having instituted the annual sports day, become scoutmaster of the Fairmile Troop, as it was known, and on the whole acted as a father to the Cottage Homes children, as Mrs Grimes observed to her fellow Public Assistance Committee members on his death in 1941 (not that she knew all that there was to know). His obituary in the local paper praised 'his kindly discipline and flair for organisation, which had raised the tone of the Homes to a high standard, the children being well-mannered and orderly'. In the light of the behaviour of his staff one wonders if there is ever any truth at all in obituaries. The obituary went on to note the prominent role he had played in the town, being a member of the town's football club and amateur dramatic society and also a singer. Mrs Dunn was to continue alone; she was the

*Workhouse corridor*

same kind of person, with public commitments over and above her position in the Homes – for many years being chairman of the Christchurch Townswomen's Guild, a Civil Defence Officer during the war, a freemason and a Red Cross worker. Sadly, the couple lost a son during the war. The reference to freemasonry is curious: time and time again membership of one Lodge or another is revealed in local obituaries in the first half of the 20th century.

Mrs Dunn according to a source who was brought up in the Homes in the forties, was an exceptionally caring person, but may have been somewhat naive about some of the other members of staff, particularly the 'Aunties' who were in charge of the individual Homes. The abuse that was coming to light earlier continued unabated. Furthermore, pilfering of supplies was apparently common, which included literally taking the sweets from the mouths of babes – their sweet rations were allegedly appropriated. Punishments were devised to humiliate children as before: bedwetters were treated as before cited. Whilst the children spent their after-school hours mending their socks before going to bed early, some of the staff amused themselves drinking in their rooms, and any bad tempers were inevitably taken out on their young charges.

My source for this information has since supplied new and even more alarming details: two of the 'Aunties' (named, to me, but not here), had physical fights in front of the children; the gardener was sinister and fond

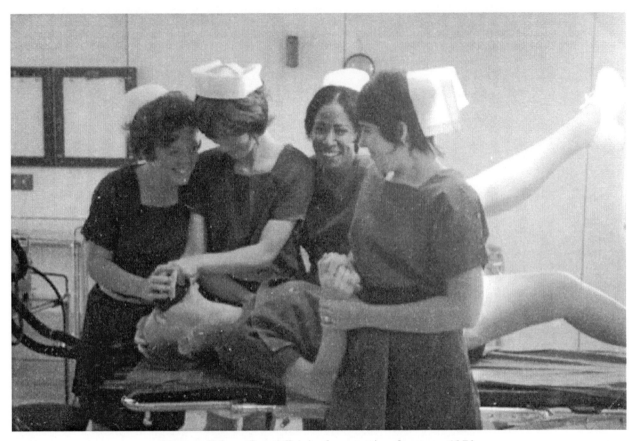

*Nurses off duty (hopefully) in the operating theatre, c. 1970*

of watching the girls being strip-washed; the shoemaker was 'quite violent' – my informant clearly recalls him beating a girl before other children; his own sister in talking over their experiences agreed it was like 'a chapter out of Dickens'. The final straw was a court case against one of the 'Aunties'.

The outside world knew none of this, of course, and regarded the children with mixed feelings, said the same informant. They seemed to suffer from a poor reputation which was undeserved, being often the first suspects at school whenever a misdemeanour was discovered; on the other hand, many kinder people would take the children on excursions, and at Christmas and Easter they received gifts galore. He singled out Canon Gay and Canon Price at the Priory Church as especially well-disposed towards he and his fellow unfortunates.

Education was provided in his day at Stourfield School in Southbourne, to which the children walked daily. This school was very good to the children on the whole, but no encouragement in their studies was given back at the Homes, as a result of which homework was rarely done and eventually not even set. Sundays were church days: a walk to the Priory, sometimes twice, and another walk to St George's in Jumpers Road. Here, of all places, in the sanctuary of a church, the children should have felt safe from abuse. Yet in 1945, the Revd Bunn, of the church, was committed to four years' penal servitude for offences against Cottage Homes boys in the church.

Life was not all grim, though grim enough. In the summer there were regular picnic excursions to the river nearby, and throughout the year the dining hall at Fairmile House was used for film shows. A weekly visit to a youth club at Pokesdown was permitted, and the big annual events such as bonfire night and sports day were eagerly looked forward to.

This brief account of life at the Homes in those days is a reminder that children's homes scandals are not a modern phenomenon. It suggests that insufficient attention was paid by the authorities to the proper training and supervision of the Cottage Homes staff, as a result of which the kind of person attracted to these posts were sometimes ill-educated and temperamentally unsuited to work that required patience and integrity.

All seemed as usual at the start of the fifties, except that the Homes had been renamed the Bournemouth Children's Homes. The outings continued much as before – a visit to Weymouth, summer camp at New Romney, Kent, a children's party hosted by the newly-formed Christchurch Lodge of the Royal Order of the Moose, and so on. But change was in the air. The closure of Home No.3 was discussed by the Children's Committee as early as 1949. The reason on the surface was the new enlightenment: children should be fostered out when at all possible. The same fate was being planned for Homes 1 and 2 not much later. Miss Isobel Maundy, the Children's Officer for the Bournemouth Council, had had enough of the outrages at the Homes. In 1944 one of the 'Aunties' had gone on trial for the theft of various items – blankets. crockery, etc – and although acquitted, the writing was on the wall. Miss Maundy's committee approached the main Bournemouth Council with the offer to hand over the Homes for use by elderly and infirm people currently clogging up the wards earmarked at the hospital for surgical cases. That sealed the fate of the Homes, and gave the hospital management authorities the solution to the problem with old people that had caused so much controversy only shortly beforehand. The end, when it came, was sudden. Mrs Dunn was offered alternative work, but none suited, and she retired, the tribute from the Children's Committee ('ability and loyalty … kindness and affection to many children …') ringing in her ears. She died in 1956. The Homes were to close to the children on 31 March 1952. The same month the Homes were rechristened Queens Close (as if to wipe out all trace of its former pauper associations, just as the redevelopment of the workhouse site opposite has been named, ludicrously, 'Regency Park'!), furniture was removed from the Elizabeth Wood Home of Rest at the hospital, lino was laid, radiators installed, and about 100 old people made the move across the road to their new hostel in July. What they felt about it history has failed to record. It was the obligation of Regional Hospital Boards to provide hostel-type accommodation for such elderly people, and hostels were in fact springing up all over the area. The responsibility for children was also defined under the 1948 Children's Act which dictated that all local authority children should be boarded out.

The coup was reported in *The Bournemouth Times*: 'Bournemouth Corporation Children's Committee has been so successful in boarding out boys and girls under their care into decent, private homes that they have been able to close down their Christchurch Cottage Homes … More than 100 young people in these Homes have been found foster-parents.' Miss Maundy commented that it showed how much Bournemouth people have supported them in their search for good homes. The children were visited regularly and strictly supervised, just as they had been since the practice was first adopted in Mr Blandford's day. Not all the children found such homes: some were in council premises in 53 Wellington Road, or 12 Suffolk Road, and some at a nursery in Southbourne. Not all escaped further abuse.

There was, of course, no use for the land and the piggeries, which were therefore let out. There was also no further use for the children's swings, which went to the Bournemouth Council's Children and Parks Committee.

Around 1957, the old schoolroom from the Cottage Homes days seems to have enjoyed a new and rather unsavoury role as the dumping ground for Bournemouth's problem families, who appear to have lived alongside whatever old people remained in the Queen's Close hostels at this time. This came to the attention of *The Christchurch Herald*. In a 'shock horror' front-page splash the paper tried to wake up Christchurch people to the prevailing situation in what was, after all, still part of Christchurch, even though it had by then been under Bournemouth for years. 'Appalling Conditions', screamed the headline, going on to make allegations about families living in sub-standard, cramped conditions, without hot water or storage facilities, with tramps from the Reception Centre prowling around at all hours. The schoolroom occupants appear to have been people evicted from Bournemouth council houses. Councillor Tucker complained in person to the Ministry of Health and returned hopeful. His optimism was somewhat excessive: all that resulted was the repair of a damaged sink and the provision of an additional refuse bin.

The first Home to have been bulldozed according to Bournemouth Council minutes was No. 4, which made way in 1965 for Avon View Old People's Home. This, reported *The Christchurch Times*, was 'raised, ironically, on the site of a provision of the Poor Law, which many people dreaded – the workhouse … The Director of Welfare Services says the cottage-type homes at Christchurch – retained only for emergency – will disappear when the second home is built …'

Next to go was No.7 – not a number ever in use, but probably the nursery, No.6. As promised, Queensmead, Old People's Home was erected in 1967. Three more Homes had gone in 1965; the Superintendent's Home (then recently let to hospital doctors) in 1966; and the last Home, No. 2, in the same year. Homes 5 and 6 were less than 40 years old, and contained fittings of high quality, as did all the workhouse structures – it seems such a waste (but thirty years later many more of the excellent former local workhouse buildings were similarly trashed). This sequence may have been put into operation in a different order than above stated, but accurate information on this point does not exist.

The buildings thus cursorily disposed of, the question remained of what to do with all the land – about 17 acres of it. Something of a wrestling match then ensued between two Bournemouth Council committees: the Housing Committee and the Welfare Services Committee. Plans for redevelopment had been discussed with the County Council (which at that time had to be approached for planning applications involving more than five acres), but Christchurch Council was unenthusiastic. The Welfare Committee claimed the value of the land if the Housing Committee acquired it; it then became an uneconomic proposition. In 1969, Bournemouth Council submitted an application for 210 homes, which was approved. 'The biggest single housing scheme in Christchurch's history', in the words of the Bournemouth planners, went ahead, and Queen's Close passed into history in favour of Bronte Avenue, Emily Close, and so forth – names as irrelevant to the previous use as could be found.

I am told by an occupant of one of the houses in Emily Close, site of Home No. 5 (for boys), that the sound of children can be heard in the empty upstairs bedroom. It is the sound of laughter, and of someone getting in and out of bed. One of the former Cottage Homes children had told me that the favourite dormitory game was climbing in and out of bed …

# Postscript

## Later hospital history

Major expansion of the hospital was launched in 1970, when £660,000 was spent in turning it into a rehabilitation and assessment centre for the Wessex Regional Hospital Board. The single-storey building between the former men's and women's infirmaries, in impersonal NHS parlance styled H and G Blocks, was the result; unfortunately the glass corridor linking them and a magnificent old chestnut tree were sacrificed in the process.

On the west side of these old infirmaries were constructed new wards for specialised purposes: Forest Dene rehabilitation unit, wards J, K, and M, the MacMillan cancer unit, and a gymnasium and hydrotherapy pool.

In 1992, the long-awaited Royal Bournemouth Hospital was opened in Castle Lane, near former Guardian Mr Cooper-Dean's mansion, Littledown House, now part of the Chase Manhattan Bank. Christchurch Hospital then lost its operating theatres.

In 1991 a Conservation Area was declared by Christchurch Borough Council to include the Master's House, the reception range and archway in Jumpers Road – all the work of Christopher Crabbe Creeke; the nurses' home, the boardroom, the three main wards – one for the females and two for the men, the workshop range and the dining hall. In 1995 permission was sought and obtained to demolish all of these buildings, with the exception of the Master's House and the Jumpers Road frontage (apart from the wonderful vagrants' wards, which were also permitted to go) which were granted permission for conversion. Soon after, the 1882 infirmary was destroyed to make way for a roundabout to serve the redevelopment area. In addition to the Conservation Area buildings which were to be demolished, and were, the children's accommodation and school, the 1898 lying-in ward, the laundry, mortuary and stables were also destroyed. In addition, half the row to the left of the archway, comprising the reception range, was torn down without planning consent. From the cleared ground providing several acres from lost heritage, arose serried ranks of 'Regency'-style terraces, and a curved and massy block for retirement apartments.

Four years further on, the Jumpers Road row is reduced to a state of dereliction, so advanced that despite the arrival of a new Director of Planning at Christchurch Council, which was taken to appeal by the developer over his application to demolish all that remains of this row, the enquiry inspector allowed demolition on account of the decay which had taken place whilst it was the property of the developer. However, the scale and density of the proposed replacement were not in his view acceptable. A year has passed since the enquiry and the decay continues apace in what is left of the original buildings of the Christchurch Hospital Conservation Area. The boardroom, although purchased by the council for community use, remains unrepaired.

The destruction of almost an entire Conservation Area was opposed not just by hundreds of local residents, but by the Victorian Society, SAVE Britain's Heritage, the Council for British Archaeology, the Ancient Monuments Society and numerous local amenity bodies, such as residents' associations, the local history society, the local civic society and so on. Only English Heritage withheld support.

A conversion scheme had been drawn up at an early stage by Huw Thomas, the brilliant architect responsible for the conversion of the Peninsula Barracks at Winchester. A buyer for the entire site had been found before the NHS sold it. That such a situation subsequently arose that led to the present state of affairs hardly does credit to a town which has the logo 'Christchurch, Where Time is Pleasant', and promotes itself heavily as a historic town when encouraging tourists. It is always a sad sight to see the loss of the fabric of our heritage in any form; in this case it was of an institution which had been involved in the lives of countless thousands of people in the two towns of Christchurch and Bournemouth, absorbed the energies and talents of the leading figures of their day in their capacity as Guardians, developed a nursing training school which became renowned not only in Christchurch or the region but internationally, and which was described by the experts from the Royal Commission on the Historic Monuments of England as 'unique'.

This second edition of *The Christchurch and Bournemouth Union Workhouse* will alone have to act as the record of the achievements of a previous set of Christchurch public servants with radically different objectives from those who have represented us in recent times, and it is some consolation that all of the first workhouse did not suffer the fate of the second, and we at least have something in the town as a reminder of the fascinating story such extraordinary buildings have to tell.

R.I.P. Christchurch Union Workhouse 1881 – 1999.

# Conclusion

It is easy for us now to look back on the days of the workhouse with a mixture of morbid fascination and amused contempt. It seems barbaric that conditions in the workhouses should have been made so unpleasant, as if the poor and disadvantaged did not have enough brutality in their daily lives without being, in effect, punished for poverty.

It would, though, be judging our forebears too harshly if we did not take into account the inadequacy, even absence, of health care which the workhouse infirmaries gradually came to redress. Nor must we ignore the service that was provided for the elderly, in the days before universal pensions, when Christchurch Workhouse became for so many the only shelter that was to be had, and was much appreciated for that.

And, looking around today, can we really feel so proud of our provision now? In every city in Britain, destitute people sleep out in the open on benches or in cardboard boxes. Some of them – a significant proportion, maybe even the majority – are discarded from mental institutions, the great Victorian asylums, which were then closed down (Knowle Hospital included), with insufficient or non-existent aftercare. The care in the community policy has directly led to murders committed by deranged ex-patients from these asylums. Is it part of the modern values of counting the cost of everything but valuing nothing?

What progress has been made from the enforced incarceration in the casual wards? Whilst our present-day tramps are not put on punitive stone-breaking work, neither do they have food and washing facilities when needed, unless a rare emergency hostel place is available.

We still have not solved the perennial problem of the able-bodied shirkers; in fact, the present benefit system makes it easy to depend on the State and give nothing in return.

Christchurch was fortunate in having Guardians of the Poor who were, on the whole, acting in the best interest as they saw it of the people in their charge, according to the values, attitudes and legislation of their times. Nowhere have I found anything on a par with the abuses exposed at other workhouses, for example, at Andover, as referred to earlier. There is no record of children actually being flogged senseless, such as happened in the workhouse from which Sir Henry Stanley absconded. The worst episode known of in the history of our workhouse, the death of John Campbell, was certainly the result of negligence, but not of sadistic cruelty or deliberate brutality.

The legacy of the Cottage Homes is more complex. Whilst evidence has been obtained of serious malpractice, such circumstances were not confined to that particular children's home. It nevertheless remains a shameful blot on the history of the town, in that countless children were left to deal with hunger, violence, intimidation, separation from siblings, various humiliations and deprivations, without any system of check in place which could have exposed their plight. It is to their lasting credit that despite their awful start in life, so many I met since the publication of the first edition of this book had nevertheless done much in their adult lives to be proud of.

Christchurch Workhouse evolved into a fine hospital, highly regarded by local people, and a very important asset to the town.

# Bibliography

## Books:

Ackermann's *Repository of Arts, Literature, Commerce, Manufacturers, Fashion and Politics* 1809
Druitt, Herbert *Christchurch Miscellany* reprinted by the Christchurch Local History Society 1996
Graham, Mary *The Royal National Hospital* 1992
Longmate, Norman *The Workhouse* 1974
Morrison, Kathryn *The Workhouse* 1999
Ruggles, Thomas *This History of the Poor* 1793
Tucker, William *Reminiscences of Christchurch and Neighbourhood* 1921 (1979 reprint)
White, Allen *The Chain Makers* 1967

## Local and national newspapers:

The Christchurch Times
The Christchurch Guardian
The Christchurch Herald
The Bournemouth Times
The Bournemouth Visitors' Directory
The Bournemouth Daily Echo
The Poole Herald
The Salisbury (later, Salisbury and Winchester) Journal
The Southampton Herald
The Christian Magazine
The London Star
Punch

## Manuscripts:

Bingley, Revd W 'History of Christchurch' 1813
Druitt, Herbert: Diaries
Mellor, John: Untitled manuscript in Local History Collection, Christchurch Library
Tunks, Peter 'The Knowle Experience' 1991

## Archive sources at:

Hampshire Record Office
Dorset Record Office
Public Record Office
Christchurch Library Local History Room
Red House Museum, Christchurch
Christchurch Hospital
Private collections

# Index

# W

# Y